FAREWELL TO INNOCENCE

FAREWELL TO INNOCENCE

A Socio-Ethical Study
on Black Theology and Black Power

ALLAN AUBREY BOESAK

ORBIS  BOOKS

Maryknoll, New York 10545

1977

Library of Congress Cataloging in Publication Data

Boesak, Allan Aubrey, 1946–
    Farewell to Innocence.

    Bibliography: p.
    Includes index.
    1. Black theology. 2. Black power. I. Title.
BT82.7.B63   1977   261.8   77-5578
ISBN 0-88344-130-6

Originally published by Uitgeversmaatachappij J.H. Kok,   -
    Kampen, Holland

Copyright © 1976 Allan Aubrey Boesak

Orbis Books, Maryknoll, New York 10545

To the memory of my father, to my mother and my wife

CONTENTS

PREFACE

Engaging in liberation theology in the South African situation is an extremely difficult, risky business. But the challenge and the message of Black Theology have struck a chord in the hearts of black people and are reverberating with a hesitant but nonetheless soulful rhythm within a community that has learned—undeniably and joyfully—the meaning of the liberating gospel of Jesus Christ.

This book was born out of the black experience in South Africa—out of anguish and deep concern; out of the inevitability of commitment; out of anger and a fragile but living hope; out of an inexplicable joy through faith in Jesus the Messiah, whose refusal to let go of me has been my liberation. I hope it is a contribution to the crucial and exciting dialogue going on between Christians of the "Third World," and between them and their brothers and sisters in the West. I do not purport to know all the answers to all the questions. I do try, however, to interpret honestly and authentically a black experience within the complexity of the meaning of blackness in South Africa. And it is from within this reality that I wish to respond to the theological articulations of brothers and sisters in North America, Asia, Latin America, and the rest of Africa.

I am deeply indebted to my many friends who have encouraged me and with whom I have had endless discussions that resulted in many helpful suggestions. I thank especially Professor Gerard Rothuizen of Kampen, Holland, and Professor Gayraud Wilmore of Colgate Rochester Divinity School, who have read the entire manuscript and have guided me with patience and admirable precision. Needless to say, the interpretation and presentation of facts are solely my responsibility.

I also want to thank other friends: Dr. Edward Huenemann, Chris Loff, Esau Jacobs, Hannes Adonis, Chris Wessels, and especially my brother, Willa—all of whom have made me see how worthwhile the struggle is.

My wife's understanding and love, her dedication and courage, make of our family life a source of genuine inspiration. I cannot even begin to tell her how much this means to me. If this work is an accomplishment, it is as much hers as it is mine.

INTRODUCTION

Farewell to Innocence

Black wisdom destroys the illusion of good masters.
                                                      James Cone

*But it is not permissible that the authors of devastation should
also be innocent. It is the innocence which constitutes the crime.*
                                                      James Baldwin

Ever since their emergence (also on the ecumenical scene) the
terms "Black Consciousness," "Black Power," and "Black
Theology" were more than merely terms. We shall define
these terms only briefly here. Black Consciousness may be
described as the awareness of black people that their humanity
is constituted by their blackness. It means that black people are
no longer ashamed that they are black, that they have a black
history and a black culture distinct from the history and culture
of white people. It means that blacks are determined to be
judged no longer by, and to adhere no longer to white values.
It is an attitude, a way of life.

Viewed thus, Black Consciousness is an integral part of
Black Power. But Black Power is also a clear critique of and a
force for fundamental change in systems and patterns in society which oppress or which give rise to the oppression of black
people.

Black Theology is the theological reflection of black Christians on the situation in which they live and on their struggle
for liberation. Blacks ask: What does it mean to believe in Jesus

1

Christ when one is black and living in a world controlled by white racists? And what if these racists call themselves Christians also?

We shall return to these terms and the questions they give rise to later on. For the moment it is enough to note that they signify a completely new phase in race relations in the world, a new psychological, social, and political reality.

Black Theology, emerging within the context of the theology of liberation, also denotes a fundamentally different approach to Christian theology, a new way of looking at the world we live in and at the responsibility of the church in the world. Black Theology signifies an irreversible reordering of the ecumenical agenda.

Of particular interest for the study of Christian (social) ethics are the consequences of the relationship between Black Theology and Black Power. It is this relationship which forms the object of our study. It all began in 1969 when James Cone opened the debate by making this bold assertion:

It is my thesis, however, that Black Power, even in its most radical expression, is not the antithesis of Christianity, nor is it a heretical idea to be tolerated with painful forbearance. It is, rather, Christ's central message to twentieth century America.[1]

In this, Cone was followed by a number of black theologians, while others criticized him severely. The discussions on these matters are of singular importance for all Christians, for they center not only on the "involvement of the church in politics," but on the authentic witness of the church to the presence of God in our history.

The ethical importance of the study of Black Theology and Black Power also becomes clear in the meaning of black theological reflection. The 1976 statement on Black Theology of the Theological Commission of the National Conference of Black Churchmen in the United States phrases it thus:

Black theological reflection takes place in the context of the authentic experience of God in the black worshipping community. That worship is and has always been about freedom under the reign of

God. . . . But the worship of the Black Church cannot be separated from its life and ethical praxis. It is in the struggle against racism and oppression that the Black Church creates and recreates its theological understanding of the faith and expresses it in shouts of praise and sounds of struggle for the liberation of the oppressed.[2]

Behind the reality of the theology of liberation and the challenge it poses for the Christian church are realities hitherto anxiously ignored by the theology of the western world—the realities of rich and poor, of white and black, of oppressors and oppressed, of oppression and liberation from oppression. Until now, the Christian church had chosen to move through history with a bland kind of innocence, hiding these painful truths behind a façade of myths and real or imagined anxieties. This is no longer possible. The oppressed who believe in God, the Father of Jesus Christ, no longer want to believe in the myths created to subjugate them. It is no longer possible to innocently accept history "as it happens," silently hoping that God would take the responsibility for human failure. The theology of liberation spells out this realization. For the Christian church it constitutes, in no uncertain terms, a farewell to innocence.

In using this term, we are guided by what psychologist Rollo May wrote in *Power and Innocence*.[3] The word "innocence" is derived from the Latin words *in* and *nocens*, literally meaning "not harmful," to be free from guilt or sin, guileless. In actions, it means "without evil influence or effect, not rising from evil intention."[4] In contrast with authentic innocence, there is another kind of innocence May speaks of: pseudoinnocence. He writes,

Capitalizing on naiveté, it consists of a childhood that is never outgrown, a kind of fixation on the past. It is a childishness rather than childlikeness.[5]

When people face issues too horrendous to contemplate, they close their eyes to reality and make a virtue out of powerlessness, weakness, and helplessness. This innocence leads to a helpless utopianism—either an idealization of the present (bad) situation, or an escapism into a "better" world other than the present one. This pseudoinnocence cannot come to terms with the destructiveness in oneself or in others and hence it actually becomes self-destructive.[6] It is this innocence which uses "the ideal" to blind people so that they do not see the atrocities of the present. It blinds, paralyzes, and cunningly uses all means at its disposal to cover up and rationalize guilt and sin. It is an innocence which, for its own justification, does not include evil. It therefore becomes demonic.[7]

Pseudoinnocence also has another function. It effectively blocks off all awareness and therefore the sense of responsibility necessary to confront the other as a human being. This leads to an inability to repent which in its turn makes genuine reconciliation impossible. When we speak of innocence in this study, we mean this pseudoinnocence.

This does not only apply to this specific study, however, but describes the whole new reality of race relations and class relations in the world and its consequences for the Christian community.

It is a farewell to innocence for white people. In order to maintain the status quo, it is necessary for whites to believe, and keep on believing, that they are innocent. They are innocent because they "just happen to have the superior position in the world," or, in some mysterious way, they have been placed in a position of leadership (guardianship) over blacks by nature, by virtue of their "superior" culture, or by God. They may thus believe themselves to have a "divine calling" vis-à-vis blacks, or to uphold "western Christian civilization."[8] In this way, *Apartheid* in South Africa is justified by Christians also because it "serves true community," "avoids friction" (which is sin), and on grounds of the myth that *Apartheid* is really based on Christian love. It must be said, however, that this "love" has a stifling, destructive character that cannot but deny the true essence of Christian love. There is no dichotomy between love and righteousness. Love creates room for justice and always seeks to do what is right for the other. It does not seek the fulfilment of self-interest but serves the other selflessly. Christian love, in the words of Paul Tillich, overcomes all separation. In the *Apartheid* ideology, however, love is expected to serve separation and alienation; indeed it becomes the very manifestation of separation. The *Apartheid* love wants to make of the white person a neighbor (for the black), but denies the black person that same indispensable human quality: to be a neighbor for the other (the white). This, it seems to us, is the pinnacle of lovelessness.[9] Viewed thus, that expressive biblical text, "there is more happiness in giving than in receiving" (Acts 20:35), becomes a privilege "for whites only."

This *farewell to innocence* means also that the traditional role of the white liberal is thoroughly re-evaluated. The question is no longer whether whites are willing to do something *for* blacks, but whether whites are willing to identify with what the oppressed are doing to secure their liberation and whether whites are aiding that liberation in their own communities.

The same applies to other relationships in the world, for example between "white" South Africa and black "homelands" and the "first" and "third" worlds. Blacks realize that liberation from colonial regimes does not automatically mean the end of all dependency and that oppression and colonialism are simply continued on another level.[10] This innocence must be exposed, for it forms the shield behind which continued exploitation hides itself.

In 1970, when the W.C.C. program to combat racism was initiated, South African Dutch Reformed Christians were told that this program had nothing at all to do with witnessing for Christ and justice, but it was, rather, "support for unrighteous deeds *against the innocent* (whites)."[11] One need not wonder why, in its judgment on the Christian Institute of Southern Africa, the South African government accused that body of "trying to inculcate a feeling of guilt among whites of South Africa."[12] It is absolutely imperative for the oppressors to preserve their innocence just as it is imperative for the oppressed to destroy it.

However, this innocence applies to blacks also in another way. In some sense, they are no less guilty than the whites. There is, after all, a great deal of truth in the saying: The greatest ally of the oppressor is the mind of the oppressed. Getting rid of an implanted slave mentality is central to the philosophy of Black Consciousness. The affirmation of one's personhood is a powerful act that constitutes a farewell to innocence. Blacks realize that their situation is not caused by a cosmic inevitability by powers beyond their control. Historical structures are created and maintained by people. Oppression is also a system.

The moment that people realize that their position in life is not simply their "lot" for which they have to thank (or to blame) God, they begin to see their own responsibility in history. History as such is being re-evaluated by black people. Assumptions taken for granted by whites are no longer uncritically accepted as valid. Demythologizing white history is part of this process.

While Martin Luther King could still speak of Thomas Jefferson, Abraham Lincoln, and the prophet Amos in one breath, blacks have come to see Lincoln (and others like him) in a new perspective, and they judge him accordingly when they hear him say: "My paramount object in this struggle is to save the Union; and it is not either to save or destroy slavery. If I could save the Union without freeing any slave I would do it; and if I could save it by freeing some and leaving others alone, I would also do that."[13]

Theologically speaking, blacks must take this responsibility and formulate in their own words their belief in God. They can no longer hide behind the theological formulas created by someone else. But moving away from the illusioned universality of western theology to the contextuality of liberation theology is a risky business, one that cannot be done innocently. There is, however, a consolation. In the search for theological and human authenticity within its own situation, Black Theology does not stand alone. It is but one expression of this search going on within many different contexts. Across the world oppressed and hopeful people share the same faith in the one Lord, one baptism, and one God who is Father of all, over all, through all, and within all (Eph. 4:5, 6). This study wishes to be a contribution to what we believe to be one of the most crucial discussions in the history of Christian theology.

While we acknowledge that all expressions of liberation theology are not identical, we must protest very strongly against the total division (and contrast) some make between Black Theology in South Africa and Black Theology in the United States; between Black Theology and African theology; between Black Theology and the Latin American theology of liberation. As a matter of principle, we have therefore treated all these different expressions within the framework where they belong: the framework of the theology of liberation. The reader who keeps this in mind, we trust, will not find illustrations from different situations confusing.

This is a study on Black Theology and Black Power. The five chapters into which it is divided follow a definite pattern, and because of the particular nature of the subject, they may sometimes overlap.

Chapter 1 examines the basis of liberation theology, at the same time establishing the framework of black theological reflection. Chapter 2 is a discussion on power with a strong emphasis on Black Power. Having determined our understanding of Black Theology and Black Power separately, in chapter 3 we turn our attention to the relationship which exists between the two. The question that obviously arises out of this discussion is this: If there is a relationship between Black Theology and Black Power, does not Black Theology become an ideology? This question is discussed in chapter 4. In chapter 5 we discuss Black Theology more fully from a specifically socio-ethical point of view. This chapter is concluded by a directive for an ethic of liberation as an ethic for Black Theology.

CHAPTER ONE

The Coming of the Black Messiah

On Theology

Is the Christian faith the acceptance of the correct interpretation of certain texts, or is the Christian faith the commitment to obedience to the Lord Jesus Christ? If it is the latter, really, the question is, how does this obedience express itself concretely, so that you really know how the text has to be understood in relation to your total Christian experience. So actually you cannot say whether you read the text correctly until you say how you treat the poor farmer. . . . This, I would say, is theology. So that really the correct interpretation of the text has to tell me how you have dealt with the poor farmer and therefore with the rich landowner who owns his work.

José Míguez Bonino

The bias is clear beyond any doubt. God sides with the oppressed. The oppressors are on the wrong side. It is as clear as that. And as disturbing as that.

Robert McAfee Brown

A BLACK THEOLOGY OF LIBERATION

Black Theology is a theology of liberation. By that we mean the following. Black Theology believes that liberation is not only "part of" the gospel, or "consistent with" the gospel; it is the content and framework of the gospel of Jesus Christ. Born in the community of the black oppressed, it takes seriously the black experience, the black situation. Black Theology grapples with suffering and oppression; it is a cry unto God for the sake of the people. It believes that in Jesus Christ the total liberation of all people has come.

Black Theology refuses to believe that the gospel is the narrow, racist ideology white Christians have made of it. Black Christians cannot believe that the last word about Christianity is that it is a "white man's religion," or a "slave religion" designed for the oppression of the poor.

The development of the philosophy of Black Consciousness in the last decade strengthened this "black Christian consciousness" even more. It is no longer possible for black Christians to escape these pressing questions: How can one be black *and* Christian? What has faith in Jesus Christ to do with the struggle for black liberation? What was (and still is) the role of the Christian church in the oppression and the liberation of blacks? When trying to answer these existential questions, it becomes abundantly clear that for blacks neither white questions nor white answers any longer suffice. Black theological reflection must take seriously precisely what Christian theology has hitherto ignored: the black situation. In its focus on the poor and the oppressed, the theology of liberation is not a new theology; it is simply the proclamation of the age-old gospel, but now liberated from the deadly hold of the mighty and the powerful and made relevant to the situation of the oppressed and the poor.

One can say that it represents a new way of theologizing, a new way of believing. Liberation theology, by beginning with the Exodus, by making of theology a critical reflection on the praxis of liberation, places the gospel in its authentic perspective, namely, that of liberation. It seeks to proclaim the gospel according to its original intention: as the gospel of the poor. In this, Black Theology seeks the God of the Bible, who is totally and completely different from the God whites have for so long preached to blacks. The God of the Bible is the God of liberation rather than oppression; a God of justice rather than injustice; a God of freedom and humanity rather than enslavement and subservience; a God of love, righteousness, and community rather than hatred, self-interest, and exploitation.

Black Theology knows that it is not merely people who need to be liberated. The gospel, so abused and exploited, also needs to be liberated. In this liberation movement through history black Christians are joyfully engaging themselves.

You're a Soul Brother, Jesus: Why Black "Theology"?

DOING THEOLOGY: SHARING THE FAITH.   Before going on to explicate in more detail what we have said above, it is necessary to state clearly our understanding of theology. James Cone sees theology as "the rational study of the being of God in the world in the light of the existential situation of an oppressed community, relating to the essence of the gospel, which is Jesus Christ."[1] For Gustavo Gutiérrez the Word of God is incarnated in the community of faith which gives itself to the service of humankind. This activity of the church as the community of faith must be the starting point of all theological reflection.[2]

On the question of why one should start with human activity, Gutiérrez answers: There is a new relationship between man and nature which affects the awareness man has of himself (and consequently, we may add, man's awareness of his role in history). Second, Gutiérrez speaks of a new focus on praxis (service) geared to the transformation of the world. And third, for Gutiérrez communion with the Lord inescapably means a Christian life centered around a concrete and creative commitment of service to others. With all this, theology comes to mean man's critical reflection on himself, on his own basic principles, a clear and critical attitude regarding economic socio-cultural issues in the life and reflection of the Christian community. Theology as critical reflection on society and the life of the church is "worked out in the light of the Word (of God), accepted in faith and inspired by a practical purpose—and therefore indissolubly linked to historical praxis."[3]

When Cone speaks of theology as "passionate language," he hints at this same involvement in historical praxis that Gutiérrez talks about,[4] but his point of departure is clearly still the "rational study." We prefer the formulation of Gutiérrez. Theology which is reflection upon action transforming the world is also faith active in the world. We understand faith not just as a confession, but as an act of trust in and commitment to God and to humanity. Faith is, in the words of Hugo Assmann, the action of love within history.[5]

If one accepts this view, as we do, one accepts that theology is not an automatic mental or spiritual process, nor merely a philosophical exercise. "We believe," states the report of a theological workshop in Asia, "that theology is not detached, cool, objective, or neutral. Theology is passionately involved. It begins with the experience of the actual struggles, suffering and joys of particular communities."[6] For black people, this means that theology must engage itself in the *black* experience, an experience shared by and articulated in a community.

We may say, thus, that theology is critical reflection on historical praxis; in other words, it is the active involvement of the church in the world. At the same time theology is faith manifested—the action of love within history. But it is a critical reflection *in the light of the Word of God*, which means that all action and all reflection is finally judged by the liberating gospel of Jesus Christ.

Cone, we have noted, speaks of reflection "in the light of the black situation." This formulation calls for caution. The black situation is the situation within which reflection and action take place, but it is the Word of God which illuminates the reflection and guides the action. We fear that Cone attaches too much theological import to the black experience and the black situation as if these realities *within themselves* have revelational value on a par with Scripture.[7] God, it seems to us, reveals himself *in* the situation. The black experience provides the framework within which blacks understand the revelation of God in Jesus Christ. No more, no less.

Theology is a living experience. It means, in the wording of the Workshop Report, "having rice with Jesus."[8] This clearly underlines the conception of theology as the product of a believing community, sharing and experiencing history with God. The theology of liberation is thus not merely "God-talk," theoretical reasoning, a *logos* about the *Theos*. It proclaims the Word, which has always been a liberating, creative deed. It is participating in the liberating activity of Yahweh who has revealed himself in Jesus the Messiah. The description of Black Theology as a christological theology, meaning that Jesus Christ is at its center, is correct. It means that the passion moving black theologians is essentially a *Passio Jesu Christi*. [9]

Thus, theology becomes a liberating activity with an openness to the world and to the future, a prophetic word, but also a prophetic manifestation of the Word. In this way, theologians of the Third World speak about "doing theology." As critical reflection under the Word of God, "it is subversive with regard to ideologies which rationalize and justify a given social and ecclesiastical order, . . . preserving [the Christian community] from fetishism and idolatry, as well as from a pernicious and belittling narcissism."[10] When, standing in this tradition, Asian Christians say, "We have had rice with Jesus," it is the same as black Christians proclaiming, "You're a Soul Brother, Jesus."

BLACK THEOLOGY. Black Theology is a situational theology. It is the black people's attempt to come to terms theologically with their black situation. It seeks to interpret the gospel in such a way that the situation of blacks will begin to make sense. It seeks to take seriously the biblical emphasis on the wholeness of life, which has always had its counterpart in the African heritage, trying to transform the departmentalized theology blacks have inherited from the western world into a biblical, holistic theology. It is part of the black struggle toward liberation from religious, economic, psychological, and cultural dependency.

One can also say that Black Theology is a contextual theology.[11] We prefer the term "contextual" to the term "indigenous." Indigenization has always been the term used to describe a white, western version of "African Theology." The way in which this has happened was not only unauthentic; it was also regarded as "harmless," "innocent." Today, it is precisely at this point that some white theologians are trying to separate Black Theology from African theology as if the two have nothing in common. In South Africa, white theologians have declared themselves prepared to "accept" Black Theology if it means "indigenization" (*verinheemsing*) of the Christian faith—something they contrast with the "revolutionary," "anti-white," and "unchristian" elements in Black Theology. Because indigenization has always meant isolation and fragmentation of groups, we fear that within the *Apartheid* context such a theology would become nothing more than a "homeland theology."[12] Indigenization has too much of a colonial aura clinging to it and has been used too one-sidedly in the sense of "response to the gospel in terms of traditional culture." Contextual theology takes this aspect fully into account—Black Theology is, after all, profoundly African, as we shall see—but it also takes seriously the processes of the struggle for humanity and justice, of secularity and technology. Response to the gospel "within the context" and response to the gospel in terms of traditional culture, however, do not have to be contradictory categories.[13]

A contextual theology must be authentic. It must not yield to uncritical accommodation, becoming a "cultural theology" or a religion of culture. An authentic contextual theology is a prophetic one; it is not merely an exhumation of the corpses of tradition as African theology was sometimes understood to be, but attempts to make critical use of those traditions from the past which can play a humanizing and revolutionizing role in contemporary society. It takes from the past what is good, thereby offering a critique of the present and opening perspectives for the future. This is a process always arising "out of genuine encounter between God's Word and his world, and moves toward the purpose of challenging and changing the situation through rootedness in, and commitment to a given historical moment."[14] It is dynamic, "giving account of the hope that is within us" in a given situation, committed always to the central message of the Bible, i.e., liberation. Black Theology is such a contextual theology.

The term Black Theology dates from 1966, when the Committee on Theological Perspectives of the NCBC in the U.S.A. wrote:

Black Theology is a theology of black liberation. It seeks to plumb the black condition in the light of God's revelation in Jesus Christ, so that the black community can see that the gospel is commensurate with the achievement of black humanity. Black Theology is a theology of "blackness." It is the affirmation of black humanity that emancipates black people from white racism, thus providing authentic freedom for both white and black people. It affirms the humanity of white people in that it says "No" to the encroachment of white oppression. [15]

This expression of Black Theology can be understood only if one understands the historical situation. All over the Third World the struggle for liberation created a new consciousness which took a specific form in every situation. [16] In America this consciousness, having been dormant for decades, was awakened especially by the work of Malcom X and Martin Luther King, Jr. And it is not at all difficult to see why it so powerfully influenced black people in South Africa and all over the world. It has in common with all the struggles in the Third World the search for identity, genuine humanity, and a truly human life.

It shares the longing to break the chains of dependency and to seek a way out of the meaningless contradiction in which oppressed people are forced to live. There is a desire to come to terms with oneself as well as with one's situation. There is a new awareness, a new self-understanding, a vision of a completely new dimension of life. This vision is represented by a truer affirmation of the black self, by a new interpretation of history, and a new analysis of the situation of oppression.

Although the term is new, Black Theology as such is not. In fact, it is as old as the attempts of white Christians to bring the gospel to blacks. Right now it represents one of the most meaningful (albeit, as Manas Buthelezi has observed, also one of the most misunderstood) events of our time. Being a theology of the poor and the oppressed, Black Theology seeks to focus on them not as marginal people, but to bring into their lives a new understanding of their liberation in Jesus Christ. It seeks to transform their blackness from its peripheral existence to the centrality of joyous life in accordance with the gospel—precisely where Jesus has placed it. It seeks to bring the gospel as a relevant message to people who have lost their self-respect, who are denied human dignity, and who are trying to come to grips with a thousand dehumanizing facets of life.

As such it is in the first place a theology for oppressed people. But not only that. It is a theology of liberation and it is this focus on liberation which makes the contextuality of Black Theology truly ecumenical and universal. In this sense, Black Theology is not an exclusive, theological *Apartheid* in which whites have no part. On the contrary, blacks know only too well the terrible estrangement of white people; they know only too well how sorely whites need to be liberated—even if whites themselves don't! Black Theology is a passionate call to freedom, and although it directs its voice to black people, it nonetheless hopes that white people will hear and be saved (Mpunzi).

LIBERATION, THE CONTENT OF BLACK THEOLOGY

It was James Cone who first focused on liberation as the central message of the gospel, and therefore of Christian theology. Authentic Christianity affirms that God is there, on the side of the oppressed, working for their liberation in their particular situation. Cone writes:

Liberation is not only *consistent* with the gospel but it is the gospel of Jesus Christ. There can be no theology which is not identified unreservedly with those who are humiliated and abused.[17]

For Cone, Black Theology does not only believe that the liberation of black people *is* God's liberation, but that blackness constitutes both liberation and oppression in any situation.[18] Blackness and oppression, and blackness and liberation are identified in Cone's thinking, not only because in the context of the United States it is blacks who are oppressed, but also because "blackness symbolizes oppression and liberation in *any* society," and in order to share in God's liberating work in the world, white people must come to ask: How can we become black?[19]

Leaving Cone's identification of blackness, oppression, and liberation for the moment, we affirm that in this respect Cone is right: The gospel of Jesus Christ *is* the gospel of liberation. Again, liberation is not merely part of the gospel, nor merely "one of the key words" of the gospel; it is the content and framework of the whole biblical message. Let us give some separate attention to this statement.

Yahweh is the Liberator—the Word is Liberation

Nothing is more central to the Old Testament proclamation than the message of liberation. God's history with Israel is a history of liberation. Yahweh's great act of liberation forms the content of the life and faith, the history and confession of Israel. As Liberator Yahweh has revealed himself to Moses and Israel, and by this name he wants to be evoked for all generations to come (Ex. 3:15). The name by which God reveals himself is YHWH—the One who is active, who is and is present, who shall free his people: "I have seen the miserable state of my people in Egypt. I have heard their appeal to be free of their slave-drivers. Yes, I am well aware of their sufferings. I mean to deliver them out of the hands of the Egyptians. . ." (Ex. 3:7,8).[20]

In the Old Testament, the Exodus, that liberating deed par exellence, is the object of the confession of Israel.[21] The so-called "Song of the Sea" (Ex. 15:1–21) is one of the oldest documents in the history of Israel.[22] It is the "first song to the new God that broke the silence of the desert" (Kaufmann). The theme of liberation is already present in Gen. 15:14 and it is evident right through the Old Testament in the preaching of the prophets as a fundamental fact of redemption. In second Isaiah not only history, but also creation, as deed of the liberating God, testifies to Yahweh's liberating power.[23] And in the most recent Old Testament book, Daniel, Daniel speaks of Yahweh as "Lord our God, who by your mighty hand brought us out of Egypt . . ." (9:15).

One can safely say that the Exodus-event is as central to the Old Testament as is the resurrection of the new,[24] even more so since the Exodus and the resurrection are not disparate, but rather they represent the same reality. The Exodus was a liberation movement in which the people of Israel were moving with God—away from meaninglessness and alienation, away from uncertainty and misery, from pain and humiliation toward service of the living God.

The Exodus is not a myth, but the opening up of history in which God's liberating act was revealed to his people. The fundamental importance of all this for Israel is best illustrated by the fact that the celebration of this event during the feast of the Passover formed the center of the liturgy of Israel. Time and time again the Exodus-event is reiterated in the Psalms; it functions as legitimization for the proclamation of social justice, and the actualization of the Exodus-event is doubtless of prime importance in the proclamation of the prophets.[25] The liberation of Israel out of Egypt is held before the people as their hope in difficult situations; it becomes the basis of the proclamation of the "new Exodus" in the ministry of the prophets. Even if it is true that the Exodus is not mentioned explicitly, the liberation of the people in that particular situation is described in terms clearly reminiscent of the Exodus.[26]

This liberation message was the center and sustenance of the life of Israel. At the heart of the liberation event is Yahweh's love for his people, manifested in his righteousness—his urge to do what is right for his people. Thus we read: "If Yahweh set his heart on you and chose you, it was not because you outnumbered other peoples. It was for love of you and to keep the oath he swore to your fathers that Yahweh brought you out with his mighty hand and redeemed you from the house of slavery, from the power of pharaoh, the king of Egypt" (Deut. 7:7).

Black Theology, taking its clue from this biblical message, refuses to let go of the truth that one cannot speak about God's love without also speaking of his righteousness, his justice, which become concrete in his relation to human beings and the relations of people among themselves. God's love for his people is a divine activity, an activity bent on doing justice to his people. His love is never a kind of sentimentality that Israel could just as well do without. It is always surprisingly concrete. Loving his people means that Yahweh takes the side of his people against the oppressor, the pharaoh. And what God does to save his people does not happen in the dark; he does it openly, thereby challenging the powers and the powerful that dare to defy him. Yahweh comes openly to the aid of his downtrodden people for all the world to see and know that he lives with and for his people, that he is the Liberator of the oppressed and the One who uprightly defends the poorest, who saves the children of those in need and crushes their oppressors (Ps. 72). He is not ashamed of being called their God: "You have seen what I have done to the Egyptians, how I carried you on eagle's wings and brought you to myself" (Ex. 19:4,5). This experience with Yahweh made the people of Israel realize that Yahweh is not just one among many gods. No, he is the only true God. He is the completely Other. And the all-surpassing characteristic of Yahweh is his acts in history as the God of justice and liberation for the sake of those who are weak and oppressed. He is the One whose love and righteousness cannot be deferred. Herein lies the incomparability of Yahweh for Israel, expressed, for example, in Ps. 82, where the gods are challenged to prove that they are indeed Gods. The test? The liberation of the oppressed, doing justice to the weak and the destitute, fairness to the orphan and no more favoring of the wicked. When these gods could not, the psalmist concluded: "I once said, 'you too are gods, sons of the Most High, all of you, but all the same, you shall die like other men; as one man, princes, you shall fall' " (6, 7). He is truly

God who sides with the weak and needy and who liberates the
oppressed. Who cannot do that is not God.[27]

We may now conclude: God's righteousness and love become manifest in his deeds of liberation. It must be clear that
Yahweh's liberation is not an isolated happening, a kind of
flash-in-the-pan that is here one day and gone the next. It is a
movement through history wherein Yahweh has proven himself to be the Liberator. He demands justice not only from the
pharaoh who oppresses Israel, but also from the rich and
powerful within Israel who will not give justice to the poor.
Not only does *He* move through history to liberate his children;
Yahweh also moves people to do his will, which is to do
justice, to love mercy, and to walk humbly with God (Micah
6:6–8). It is not entirely accidental that the text cited from Ex. 19
is followed almost immediately by Ex. 20: "I am YHWH your
God, who brought you out of the land of Egypt, out of the
house of slavery." This liberating activity cannot be separated
from God's love: "When Israel was a child I loved him, and I
called my son out of Egypt" (Hos. 11:1).

The Gospel of the Poor

Just as in the Old Testament, the message of liberation forms
the *cantus firmus* of the proclamation of the New Testament.[28]
Jesus did not alienate himself from the prophetic proclamation
of liberation. In the New Testament, everything centers
around the fact that the Messiah, the Promised One, has come.
The ministry of Jesus does not only fulfill the prophecies of the
Old Testament; it also points to the future and thereby opens
up eschatological perspectives for the community for the
faith.[29] Jesus purposely places himself in the prophetic tradition of preaching the liberation message, offering himself as
the fulfilment of the messianic prophecies. This is especially
clear in his first sermon in the synagogue of Nazareth, an event
described in Luke 4. This text lies at the heart of the theology of
liberation. Let us take a closer look at the text:

The Spirit of the Lord has been given to me,
for he has anointed me.

He has sent me to bring good news to the poor,
to proclaim liberty to the captives
and to the blind new sight,
to set the downtrodden free,
to proclaim the Lord's year of favor.

There has been a remarkable discomfort among most western commentators insofar as they have taken any notice of this passage.[30] Comment offered generally runs along the following lines: The proclamation of the good news in the preaching of Jesus is of purely spiritual significance. The terms "poor," "captives," "blind," "oppressed" must be seen, so it is argued, in their "inward, spiritual sense." These terms represent, according to these exegetes, "categories" which designate those who are victims of inward repressions, neuroses, and other spiritual ills due to misdirection and failure of life's energies and purposes.[31] The cure offered by Jesus is "the secret of salvation" in a purely spiritual sense.

Quite from another angle, but with the same disastrous results, H. Conzelmann argues that this passage (Luke 4:18–21) is a "typical piece of Lucanic theology" and therefore not of conclusive theological import to this text.[32] Conzelmann insists that Luke looks back on the life of Jesus as the central epoch of *Heilsgeschichte*. In other words, the life of Jesus was the period of the manifestation of salvation, a period in which Satan is far away. This gives the ministry of Jesus an extra emphasis in the interpretation of Luke, which gives rise to distinctive features in Luke's presentation of Jesus, e.g., 4:18–21. These distinctive features are linked to Luke's theological perspective. G. N. Stanton, in his study *Jesus of Nazareth in New Testament Preaching*, states that "serious criticisms can be levelled against this viewpoint of Conzelmann." He holds that

Luke looks back to the past of Jesus not because it was an idyllic period of salvation, but because the story of Jesus of Nazareth is the story of the fulfilment of God's promises, a story which began with the coming of Jesus and John, and which, through the Spirit, continues.[33]

Careful analysis of the gospel of Luke proves Stanton correct. We contend that the aforementioned explications deny the deepest meaning of the message of Jesus. They have nothing at all to do with the gospel of the poor. One looks in vain for a message to the people for whom Jesus meant these words in the first place. Its lack confirms what has been stated repeatedly by black theologians: The situation of blackness, of being oppressed, was never taken seriously by western Christian theology. The tendency to spiritualize the biblical message is still dominant. We are in full agreement with Gutiérrez when he warns that this excessive spiritualization is something we should profoundly distrust. It stems from a western, dualistic pattern of thought foreign to biblical mentality. "This is," he says, "a discarnate spirituality, scornful of all earthly realities."[34]

What is described in Luke 4:18–21 is a fulfilment through liberating, historical events which in turn are new promises marking the road *toward* total fulfilment.[35] We face here the problem of the "now" and the "not yet" of the kingdom of heaven. It is remarkable that the gospel does not itself explicitly distinguish between the kingdom *now* and the kingdom *later*. There is a unity in presentation which is based on the Person to whom this kingdom has been given. Keeping this unity in view is one of the fundamental presuppositions for the understanding of the gospel: In Jesus the fulfilment is there, and yet it is still to come.[36] Gutiérrez's dictum points not only toward Jesus, but also to the church and the responsibility of those who confess him as Lord, and it is in this direction we will have to seek to find at least part of the answer.

Returning to our text, we note the following: Jesus himself gives us no reason to suspect that what he had in mind should be understood in a purely spiritual sense. Close examination of the text bears this out. Jesus is the *Anointed One*, with "anointed" in the aorist, meaning once for all. "He has sent me" changes to the perfect tense, which allows us to read: He has sent me and I am here. This underlines both the definite character of his coming and the importance of his presence.[37] The *poor* Jesus was speaking of can only be understood as those who are materially poor in the first place, in other words, those who die of hunger, who are illiterate, who are exploited by others, those who do not even know that they are being exploited, who are denied the right to be persons. Manas Buthelezi speaks of the poor as those who are kept in a position where they cannot receive the (material) gifts of God.[38] The word for *prisoners* means "prisoners of war" and is used here in the sense of "captives of war," "captives who live in exile." The *blind* denote those in captivity blinded by their captors or by long imprisonment in a dungeon. Moreover, this same word *(tuphlos)* is used to describe the man born blind in John 9.[39]

The spiritualization we have indicated not only compartmentalizes life, but also leads to a distortion of the gospel message which then serves to sanction unjust and oppressive structures and relations. It forces Jesus and his message into a western, white mould, degrades him to a servant of mere self-interest, identifies him with oppression. It makes of the gospel an instrument of injustice instead of the expectation of the poor.

But there is more to be said. We have already pointed out that the whole Old Testament message is given its meaning by the liberation-event. The Year of the Jubilee and the Sabbatical Year are of particular significance in this regard. The expression used by Jesus, "to proclaim liberty," occurs in the Old Testament in a specific context, that of the Jubilee Year. Both the Jubilee and the Sabbatical Year were totally undergirded by the Exodus (Lev. 25:55).

In the proclamation of the prophets we repeatedly find references to the Jubilee, not only as judgment (for in Israel, it seems, very little was done about the Jubilee), but also as a promise and messianic prophecy. This was a reminder to Israel that it was not only a liberated people, but essentially a community which could not exist except through living the reality of liberation. In this way the Jubilee returns in the preaching of the prophets in Isa. 61:1; in Jer. 34:8, and 13–17; and finally in Ezek. 46:17. It is this prophetic proclamation which Jesus applied to himself in his first message in the

synagogue of Nazareth. Bearing in mind that a New Testament reference to an Old Testament verse is very often intended to evoke the whole passage (and its context) from
which it had been selected, it becomes clear that this passage
ties together the main thrust of Isa. 61:1, Isa. 58, Isa. 52:7, and
Ps. 107:20. These passages alluded to in Luke 4:18–21, writes
G. Stanton,

are not random choices, but seem to have been woven together to
provide a scriptural summary of the nature and significance of the
ministry of Jesus.[40]

The particular character of this holy year, writes B. Maarsingh, apart from the rest for the land, lies in the proclamation
of *deror*.[41] This term is related to the Accadic terms *andurara*,
durara, which stem from *dararu*: "letting go," "release," "to
live freely," "to move about." In all of these terms the emphasis is on *movement*. They are dynamic rather than static. In
later prophetic preaching, *deror* signifies the liberation of
slaves (Jer. 34), the return of the exiles (Isa. 61), and the return
of property to the original owner (Ezek. 46). All this, according
to Maarsingh, is not unusual for the Mesopotamic world,
except that in Israel the proclamation of *deror* is far more radical
than elsewhere. "You will proclaim the fiftieth year holy, and
proclaim liberty *to all the inhabitants of the earth*" (Lev. 25:10). In
Israel the benefits of the holy year are meant for all, not just the
happy few. In Israel this represents a redemptive event that
cuts decisively into the social and political order. It is a liberating deed which creates room for reconciliation, for the
return of true community and authentic humanity. It is this
message, tirelessly proclaimed by the prophets, which Jesus
Christ takes as point of departure for his ministry. It is the
gospel of the poor. Jesus' ministry is the fulfilment of God's
time. The kingdom of God has come near. The movement of
liberation, begun in the Old Testament, has been given a new
dimension. Jesus' proclamation cannot be understood properly unless seen against the background of the Torah and the
Prophets.[42] In Jesus the universality of God's liberation comes

to the fore, not only for Israel, but for all people (Titus 2:11). Jesus the Messiah is the fulfilment of the promise of Yahweh to Abraham that in him all the nations of the earth shall be blessed.

With regard to the ministry of Jesus, we are reminded of this valuable insight of H. N. Ridderbos: ". . . that which is preached by the proclamation of the gospel is not only a word, but a deed, not only a sound, but reality."[43] Here Ridderbos correctly underlines the significance of the proclamation of the kingdom as the gospel of the poor which promises liberation and wholeness, justice and consolation in a most remarkable way. To spiritualize this reality is to invite heresy. Once again we stress that when Jesus speaks of the poor, he does not merely indicate "sinners" in a transcendent-ethical ideal of being, nor does he indicate a simple moral imperfection. When Jesus speaks of the poor, he speaks of them in the Old Testament sense, and when he mentions the poor as in Luke, or "the poor in spirit" as in Matthew, he is speaking of the same people. Thus we conclude with Ridderbos:

These "poor" or "poor in spirit" [the meek] appear again and again in the Old Testament, particularly in the Psalms and in the Prophets. *They represent the socially oppressed, those who suffer from the power of injustice and are harassed by those who only consider their own advantage and influence.* They are, however, at the same time those who remain faithful to God and expect their salvation from his kingdom alone.[44]

Ridderbos goes on to voice his clear opinion that the words from Luke's version of the Sermon on the Mount ("you who weep now" and "you who hunger now"—Luke 6:21) refer to the social position of the weepers, the laughers, etc., in the world, not to their moral qualities.[45]

We fully agree and hasten to point out yet a further remarkable aspect of the holy years—something that was characteristic of the ministry of Jesus: the totality, the wholeness of God's liberation. The Jubilee and Sabbatical Year are characterized by total commitment to Yahweh; the sociopolitical liberation of the poor and the oppressed becomes the demand of justice; the care for the animals is not left out and a period of rest is required for the land. There is not a single aspect of the life of Israel that is not confronted with the demand for liberation. This is what Black Theology calls "the wholeness of life" and "total liberation." This is the scope within which the gospel should be understood, proclaimed, and lived.

WHAT'S IN A NAME? WHY "BLACK" THEOLOGY?

The Concept of Blackness

Up till now we have spoken time and again of the "black situation," the "black experience," and "blackness." We have alluded to the relationship between Black Theology and Black Consciousness. In simple terms, Black Consciousness means that black people realize that the recognition of their blackness is essential to their humanity. In its relation to Black Theology, Black Consciousness means that being black becomes a decisive factor in black people's expression of their belief in Jesus Christ as Lord.

Blackness is a reality that embraces the totality of black existence. To paraphrase a central passage in *The Message to the People of South Africa*[46]: People's blackness dooms them to live the life of second-class citizens. It determines who their friends may be, whom they can marry, what work they can do and that the work they eventually do is considered inferior to that of white people. Their blackness determines that if they do the same jobs as white people they get paid less. It not only determines what education they can get; it often means that they will get no education at all. It determines whose hospitality they may accept, or to whom they may extend hospitality, if they are in a position to do so. It determines where they can get medical treatment, *if* they are fortunate enough to live in an area where they will not die of malnutrition and neglect before they reach the age of five. It determines their whole life, every single day. It means living in constant fear, always being dehumanized and humiliated, at the "mercy" of people who for three hundred years have shown in so many ways that they do not *know* the meaning of the word.

To be black in South Africa means to be classified as a "non-white": a non-person, less than white and therefore less than human. Blackness spells shame. Pastor Zephania Kameeta has summed up the feeling of millions of blacks very succinctly when, after being released from prison, he wrote in an open letter to friends: "In this country you can be a Christian ten thousand times over but if you are not white you are treated like a dog."[47]

Thus, all of life is defined within the limits of black situational possibilities. To this situation, with its pain and frustrations, its joys and secret hopes of redemption, traditional Christian theology has not even begun to address itself. Black Theology, by taking this situation seriously, seeks to realize the true humanity of black people.

For blacks, authentic humanity means *black* humanity. Blacks know that racial fellowship and reconciliation will never become a reality unless whites learn to accept blacks as *black people.* This much must be clear: When blacks speak of the affirmation of their blackness, this does not mean a resigned acceptance. It is an affirmation: *Black is Beautiful!* For people to become authentically black, to affirm their blackness in a situation where they have been taught from childhood to accept their "coloredness" or "non-whiteness" or whatever white law wishes to impose upon them, is an experience similar to a rebirth, a total conversion, the participation in the creation of a new humanity. Although this blackness we speak of is certainly, among other things, a matter of the color of the skin, it is also more than merely that, if only because not all who share blackness as color of skin are also truly *black.* This blackness is an awareness, an attitude, a state of mind. It is a bold and serious determination to be a person in one's own right.[48]

Blackness in these terms is indeed more than skin color. "Even though it is a symbol that arises from the historic meaning attached to black skin color in western civilization, it points beyond mere color to the solidarity in suffering and struggle of the descendants of all enslaved and colonized people."[49] When blacks learn to say farewell to the non-white mentality that has, after centuries, almost become second nature to them, when they learn to see that black identity is exactly the opposite of what the white system and its slaves would have them believe, then the gateway to true reconciliation is open. In this context Black Theology has spoken of the necessity of black self-love.

This should not be interpreted as "love for black, hatred for white." Jesus, in saying, "love your neighbor *as yourself,*" did indeed not prescribe a law. He does no more than accept a normal fact of life. All normal human beings have regard for themselves, have self-respect, and are aware of their worth as human beings.[50] In this sense, self-love is not sinful. We point out, furthermore, that self-love can be mentioned only within the context that Jesus himself had placed it, namely, the context of love for the other. Only then is self-love meaningful and authentic, for the neighbor is not served by the elimination of the person who ought to love him. Therefore, self-love cannot exist as an objective, independent entity. It can be understood only as an expression of the interrelated reality of human existence. Self-love should be a joyous affirmation of the desire to be there for the other in a genuine, human way. An understanding of self-love as egotism, self-interest, and the satisfaction of one's own desires at the cost of others is a distortion. Indeed, the words of Jesus are appropriate here: "He who wants to save his life shall lose it; he who loses his life for my sake shall gain it."

Self-denial is not the same as self-hatred and self-destruction, and it is these which can arise within circumstances so devastating that even basic human self-love is absent. People's personhood can be so effectively undermined, even destroyed, that in time they learn to despise themselves and regard themselves as incapable of leading normal, human lives. This abnormal situation, provided it lasts long enough, becomes for them the accepted, normal way of life. When this happens, any meaningful relationship with others is effectively ruled out. In such a situation, it is necessary to repeat the words of Jesus not merely as an affirmation, but as a divine demand.

This is the situation in which black people find themselves. Slavery, domination, injustice; being forced to live a life of contradiction and estrangement in their own country and "in exile," where fear and the urge to survive made deception a way of life; being denied a sense of belonging; discrimination—all these were realities which have almost completely broken down the sense of worth of black personhood.[51] "The slave trade," said Mr. Grosvenor in the British House of Commons in 1791, "was not an amiable trade, but neither was the trade of a butcher an amiable trade, and yet a mutton chop was, nevertheless, a very good thing."[52] A wound that has scarred the soul does not heal easily. Blacks, through Black Theology and Black Consciousness, now seek their authentic humanity, free from the blemish of white contempt—systemic or personal. Thus, black self-love does not mean that blacks "inevitably" have to hate white people as Major Jones seems to think.[53] It does mean, however, that black people will no longer accept a "brotherhood" when the one "brother" is master of the other. This kind of hypocrisy and unauthenticity that dares call itself Christian, blacks deem intolerable. White values will no longer be regarded as the highest good; white definitions will no longer be automatically accepted as valid.

To ask blacks to love themselves is to ask them to hate oppression, dehumanization, and the cultivation of a slave mentality. It is to ask them to know that they are of infinite worth before God, that they have a precious human personality worthy of manifestation. It is to ask them to withstand any effort to make them believe the opposite. So it is not hatred of white people that blacks have. It is white oppression they hate. And hate it they must. With all their hearts.

Blacks know with realistic clarity that white people, as long as they are oppressors, can never be brothers. They are the enemy. With eyes cleared by pain (Harding), blacks look beyond the limitations of oppression and inhumanity to see the open possibilities of reconciliation and genuine community. This is grace and as such it can never be cheap.

All this represents, once more, a process of real *metanoia*, conversion: for blacks, in order to become reconciled with themselves, but also for whites, to become reconciled with *themselves* and to accept blackness as authentic humanity. This is sharing in God's creation, participating in a new Exodus, creating a new black being, thereby demythologizing white superiority and humanizing white living from its own idolatrous absurdity and black living from its own blasphemous non-beingness.

Black History and Christian Theology

Black Theology is a critique of theology and ideology. Authentic critique concerns itself not only with individuals, but with traditions and systems; not only with history but also with the present. Black history, in as far as it is also white history, can be described as one of enmity, slavery, and colonialism, factors which still have their influence in contemporary society. Moreover, the Christian church and Christians have been and still are deeply involved in the subjugation and exploitation of people around the world.[54] The dictum of Gollwitzer, "the sins of our fathers are still today our profit," is extremely well put. A very brief historical survey is necessary.

Before the Constantinian period, the Christian church was a band of people, ethnically and socially mixed, politically neither influential nor powerful. When under Constantine Christianity became a state religion, however, the church changed. From then on, church and state would be allies. The confession of the church became the confession of the state, and the politics of the state became the politics of the church. The politics of the kingdom of God would henceforth be subjected to the approval of Caesar. G. J. Heering spoke of "the fall of the Christian church"[55] and rightly so. In simple terms, we might say the church became a white church, and subsequent history would prove it.

For the first time in the history of the church there was mention of a "Christliche Abendland"—meaning Europe. This tendency was strengthened after North Africa was taken over by Islam. Helmut Gollwitzer describes the events in sequence: first the Christian crusades, then the outreach of "Christian Europe" into Asia and Africa. When discussing the division of the "new world" (Latin America) between the two main Christian powers of the time, Spain and Portugal, Gollwitzer, significantly, speaks of "an Auschwitz many times over."[56] Once the Christian church had discovered what could be done with its new-found economic and political power, there was no stopping its sharing fully in all the benefits, including slavery, provided by what Gollwitzer calls the "capitalistic revolution."[57]

What must be considered one of the most significant events in the history of the Christian church, the Reformation, bypassed completely the black situation, and neither the Roman Catholic church nor the new Protestant churches endeavored to make black reality part of the fundamental changes which had occurred then. Indeed, the Reformation did not change anything about the lot whites had prepared for black people. Consider what Gollwitzer writes:

Whether Rome won or Wittenberg or Geneva; whether it was to be justification through good works or by faith; whether the Decrees of Dordt or the Statements of the Remonstrants were to become the official church doctrine; whether Cromwell or Charles I would be the victor—for the red, yellow, and black people of the world this was all irrelevant. This had no bearing whatsoever on their situation. . . . Nothing of all this would stop the capitalistic revolution as the revolution of the white, Christian, Protestant peoples that would spread all over the world to open the era of slavery which even today (albeit not in the same form) is not yet ended.[58]

And while the slave trade flourished and the destruction of black civilizations, the annihilation of the human dignity of millions, and the genocide of the Indian people continued, what did the Christian church do? How did the white, Protestant churches react? They, wrote C. Amery, became part of an especially aggressive, intolerant power, using everything from missionaries to gunboats, from development aid to napalm, to become lords of the rest of this planet.[59]

In Holland they fought each other bitterly over the doctrine of predestination. In England Puritans condemned Anglicans and Catholics to the eternal fires of hell. In South Africa Reformed Christians guarded jealously the purity of Reformed doctrine and split churches on the issue of hymns and Psalms. But when it came to the destruction of blacks, and to making their own kind of hell in America, they were all of one mind.

Slavery must be singled out as one of the most important factors in the process of the dechristianization of the church. It was also the one issue largely responsible for the breaking up of white solidarity in this process. The justification of slavery can be divided roughly into four phases:

1. In the first phase the defendants of slavery were so on morally neutral grounds.
2. Since the efforts to evangelize the slaves, however, opposition within white, Christian circles became stronger, stirring, to some measure, some people's consciences. Then biblical arguments were sought and found.
3. In the third phase slavery was defended on economic grounds and maintained, even when people began to understand that it was morally indefensible. A London publicist expressed no solitary opinion when he wrote in 1764:

   The impossibility of doing without slaves in the West (Indies) will always prevent this traffic being stopped. The necessity, the absolute necessity, then, of carrying it on, must, since there is no other, be its excuse.[60]

   Slavery was a necessity; slaves were property and as such valuable and necessary for a stable economy. While it can be said that many clergymen, and some politicians like Wilberforce, never fully accepted this view, the culture they defended certainly did.
4. In the last stage slavery was defended as a positive good, "the best solution for all concerned."

While these different phases cannot completely be separated from one another and they continually overlap, religion must be emphasized as one of the most ineradicable factors. One reason is that slavery, as already pointed out by Gollwitzer, was made a truly lucrative business by believers (Muslims as well as Christians). A second reason is that throughout history, then as well as now, religion has proven to be one of the most effective means of control and subjugation. It is not necessary to discuss this issue at length; others have done that well enough. We need no more than highlight a few instances to prove our point.

Both Gayraud Wilmore and Major Jones mention the so-called slave catechisms used in the religious instruction of blacks[61] whereof here is an example:

Question: Who gave you a master and a mistress?
Answer: God gave them to me.
Q: What did God make you for?
A: To make a crop.
Q: What is the meaning of: "Thou shalt not commit adultery"?
A: To serve our heavenly Father and our earthly master, obey our overseer and not steal anything.

There were more than enough theologians who were willing to explain that slavery was the will of God. The Bishop of London declared that according to Scripture it made no difference at all if slaves became Christians. On the contrary [!], their position remained unchanged. Clergymen like the Rev. Richard Ferman held that "the right of holding slaves is clearly established in the Holy Scriptures, both by precept and example. . . . Neither the letter nor the Spirit [!] of Scripture demands the abolition of slavery."[62] On the other hand it must be mentioned that whenever a clergyman did turn against slavery, he usually was not listened to. Dr. Porteus, another Bishop, in 1783 had preached against slavery to the Society for the Propagation of the Gospel. In the next year the Society decided to forbid Christian instruction to slaves.[63]

To what unbelievable depths of human estrangement such

attitudes could lead is known by the way these same Christians treated their slaves. Rev. P. Huet, who worked in the Transvaal in South Africa during the latter half of the previous century, described the incredible situation in Transvaal at that time.[64] Rev. Huet is all the more reliable for he does not hesitate to indict with equal indignation his own people (the Dutch) for their conduct in this same matter. Speaking of the way white Christians treated their black slaves, Huet wonders:

How is it possible that there could be any religious, or let me say, human feeling in people who force their servants, mostly children of blacks, shot dead, to sleep outside without any protection whatsoever in these cold nights, so that these unhappy wretches cover themselves with ashes, thereby inflicting upon themselves terrible burns. . . . How can there be any religious or even human feeling in people, big strong men, who will mercilessly beat these children with whips at the slightest reason, or even without any reason at all. . . . God knows, and I myself know, what indescribable injustices occur in these parts! What gruesome ill treatment, oppression, murder![65]

The active cooperation of Christian theology on the one hand and the appalling silence and indifference on the other with regard to this history, are in themselves judgment and condemnation. It is therefore of singular import to note that some western theologians are now taking cognizance of these historical facts. This is a delicate but liberating business.

The factors we have mentioned above can be applied to the *apartheid* situation in South Africa even today, and again it must be noted that the theological root of this system is not merely coincidental, for *apartheid* has always been theologically justified.

Indeed, it has been described (by defenders of the policy!) as a policy devised by the white Dutch Reformed Church.[66] In 1947, one year before the present ruling party in South Africa, the Nationalist Party, came to power, Prof. E. P. Groenewald, a New Testament scholar of the Dutch Reformed Church, made a study of the theological grounds for *apartheid*.[67] He arrived at the following conclusions:

1. Scripture teaches the unity of mankind.
2. The history of the tower of Babel (Gen. 11) teaches us, however, that when people came together to "preserve the unity of mankind" it was God himself who, according to his sovereign will, created the "separateness" of people, establishing not only "separate peoples" (nations), but also separate geographical areas and boundaries for each.
3. The event in Babel is underlined by Pentecost (Acts 2) and also in Acts 4:17.
4. In a separate paragraph entitled "It is God's will that separate peoples should maintain their separateness," Groenewald makes the identification of Israel and the Boere (Afrikaner) nation. Quoting Deut. 7:2–4 he writes: "[Purity of blood] is as necessary for a nation to do the will of God as is holiness (separateness) for the individual if he wants to serve God wholeheartedly."
5. If a nation guards its separateness (and therefore its purity of blood), it will enjoy the blessings of God.
6. Galatians 4 teaches us that the strong (the whites) have a responsibility to the weak (the blacks). In order to organize this relationship properly, two things are necessary. One is "responsibility in love" of white toward black; the other is the exercise of authority and piety. In other words, whites have the duty to excercise their love toward blacks—that is authority, because blacks are the subjugated (*onderworpe*) people. Blacks, in turn, should honor and respect whites for doing that—that is piety. "It may be expected," writes Groenewald, "that the immature people shall subject itself willingly to the authority placed over it."[68]

In 1974, so many years later, the General Synod of the white Dutch Reformed Church would again find biblical grounds for *apartheid*. A comparison with what had been written in 1947 will prove that essentially not much has changed. On the contrary, the *apartheid* policy of the present white government was once more given divine sanction: "Under certain circumstances and conditions the New Testament does leave room for organizing the co-existence of different nations in one

country *through the policy of separate development.*"[69] This is by
no means a vicious circle, it is a downward spiral.

Black History and Black Theology

The previous section of our discussion confined itself to black
history in relation to white Christianity. What then is the
relation between Black Theology and black history? This is also
part of the answer to the question: how African is Black Theology? Our thesis is that there has always been a distinct black
understanding of Christianity and the message of the Bible.

It is, we contend, wrong to suggest that Black Theology is
the product of the (white) "theology of revolution," as some
white theologians have claimed. The theology of revolution,
they argue, was conceived by the (white) World Council of
Churches in 1966 at its conference on "Church and Society."
In America, this was supposed to have been translated into a
Black Theology and imported into South Africa by a white
man.[70] Not only has there been Black Theology (or at the very
least the *Sache* of Black Theology) for as long as white Christians have been preaching the gospel to blacks, there have
always been rather strong ties between black Christians in
South Africa and the United States. One can say that being
from Africa, blacks in America have drawn on their African
religious resources until such time as they had developed their
own understanding of Christianity. Moreover, John Mbiti
states that the Christian message, on coming to African peoples, found a well-established notion that God rescues people
even when all help is exhausted, and that this rescue is primarily from material and physical dangers which confront the
individual and the community.[71] Two responses to the proclamation of the gospel were possible. One was, writes Mbiti,
that Africans would reject it if it did not penetrate into these
areas which, in their experience, called for "salvation."
Another was that they could accept the gospel and force it to fit
into whatever needed "redemptive" application.[72] Mbiti
writes:

Thus it is the experience of faith in the God of might and power, which mediates acts of redemption and salvation from those forces which work against the physical integrity of the individual and the community. Jesus is the human concentration of that divine power which heals the sick, casts out spirits, cleanses from sorcery and witchcraft, renews life, abolishes death, conquers and protects from all evil powers both human and cosmic. In effect the earthly ministry of Jesus, as directed to the physical needs of his audience, now spans two thousand years and becomes alive in African Christians, howbeit through faith in, rather than sight of, the redeemer.[73]

It is this peculiar understanding of the gospel that has influenced profoundly the black struggle for liberation. Gayraud Wilmore, in his study on black religion, confirms our thesis. He writes:

Blacks have used Christianity not as it was delivered to them by segregated white churches, but as its truth was authenticated to them in the experience of suffering, to reinforce an ingrained religious temperament and to produce an indigenous religion oriented to freedom and human welfare.[74]

In this quotation Wilmore correctly stresses not only the mistrust blacks have always had with regard to the white interpretation of the gospel (see the Independent Churches!), but also the African roots of what was to become radical Black Christianity in the United States. This black understanding of the gospel meant not only that blacks believed that the gospel and Jesus Christ were all about liberation; they also refused to believe that the biblical message could be anything else than that. We believe that this fact, more than anything else, is at the heart of the black Independent Church breakaways from the established churches. Black Christians, it seems, have always known what the central message of the gospel was, and if it was impossible for them to find it in the preaching of the white missionaries, they looked for it on their own:

They were fully aware that the God who demanded their devotion and the Spirit that infused their secret meetings and possessed their souls and bodies in the ecstasy of worship was not the God of the slave master with his whip and gun, nor the God of the plantation preacher with his segregated services and unctuous injunction to humility and obedience.[75]

White theology and the white segregated church could never give the answers to the urgent existential questions of black people, simply because these questions could not even be asked. But even so, the efforts of white people (and even missionary societies!) to bar blacks from religious instruction, in spite of religion having been used so effectively as opiate for blacks, made blacks suspect (and rightly so) that there was something so dynamic, a truth so explosive and liberating in the gospel message, that it was worth embracing and making their own. Here lie the roots of Black Theology.

This conviction was voiced again and again throughout black history. In America, Frederick Douglass, fearless abolitionist and black editor of the "North Star," in 1846 wrote:

I love the religion of our blessed Savior. I love that religion which comes from above, in the wisdom of God which is first pure, then peaceable, gentle, . . . without partiality and without hypocrisy. . . . I love that religion that makes it the duty of its disciples to visit the fatherless and the widow in their affliction. I love that religion that is based upon the glorious principle of love to God and love to man, which makes its followers do unto others as they themselves would be done by. . . . It is because I love this religion that I hate the slave-holding, the woman-whipping, the mind-darkening, the soul-destroying religion that exists in America. . . . Loving the one I must hate the other; holding to one I must reject the other.[76]

Likewise Isaiah Shembe, leader of one of the great Independent Churches in South Africa, at the end of the previous century:

You, my people, were once told of a God who has neither arms nor legs, who cannot see, who has neither love nor pity. But Isaiah Shembe showed you a God who walks on feet and who heals with his hands and who can be known by men. A God who loves and has compassion.[77]

This, in our opinion, is also Black Theology. So was the theology of Bishop Henry McNeal Turner, summed up in the phrase: "God is a Negro!" (in 1894). So was the theology of the black Independent Churches, incorporating almost from the beginning the idea of the Black Messiah and making the Exodus-event central to their preaching;[78] and so was the theology of Theodore Weld, when in 1834 it brought him to realize that there is only one way to speak of God, namely as "God of the Oppressed."[79]

The intensive contact between black Christians in South Africa, especially those belonging to the Independent Churches, and blacks in America resulted in the establishment of the African Methodist Episcopal Church (the church of Bishop Turner) in South Africa. This influence to and fro, and the acceptance both in the U.S.A. and in South Africa of black theological thinking, are proven, rather unexpectedly, by no less than Abraham Kuyper, that famous Dutch Calvinistic theologian. In a booklet on South Africa he expresses his alarm about the fraternization of black Christians of both countries, and adds with fiery indignation:

And don't think that Christianity has weakened the racial hatred of these blacks. . . . They still dream of deposing whites of their supreme power. For them, Abel was *black* and the curse of God on Cain was surely this: He made him *white!*[80]

The black struggle for liberation has always been rooted in the conviction that it is just, for if God would be anywhere, he must be on the side of the oppressed.[81] This relation between the black struggle for liberation and Black Theology has only seldom been severed. It has been kept alive by the black church movement which was begun in South Africa by Nehemiah Tile and in America by Richard Allen. It has been kept alive in the struggle for sociopolitical freedom from Maugau Mokone to Albert Luthuli; from Hendrik Witbooi in Namibia to Martin Luther King in America. Basically today, this fact has not yet changed.

It was this conviction, based on the liberating gospel of Jesus

Christ, which made Henry Highland Garnett voice his famous call for resistance.[82] Man, he argued in 1834, was created in the image of God and as such has infinite worth and dignity. Therefore, slavery and obedience to God are two things that cannot be reconciled. Slavery is not only subservience; it is also idolatry. It means that one human being is degraded to a subhuman status while the other must deify himself in order to justify his superior position. It is this sin, in both the slave and the slave master, which God will not forgive. Here no compromise was possible; slavery had to be destroyed.

In Namibia, then German South-West Africa, Hendrik Witbooi took up the struggle against the powerful Germans. Church historian J. L. de Vries writes of his struggle: "The liberation of the people of God as recorded in the Old Testament was the living example of the freedom struggle in South West Africa."[83] In his first confrontation with the German missionaries, Witbooi held onto his conviction that he should obey God more than men.[84] "Even the white people," Hendrik Witbooi wrote to Hermanus van Wyk, "shall one day have to acknowledge the Lordship of God."[85]

It must be palpably clear by now: A black liberation theology shares a common basis with African theology (and Latin American theology of liberation). The search for true and authentic human identity and liberation is also to acknowledge that one's Africanness is a God-given blessing to delight in rather than a fate to be lamented. Moreover, African theology wishes to be no more than the reflection of African Christians in the light of the Word of God, on the African situation, on African culture and traditions, on the African past and the African present. And again, this is a reflection which begins with the liberation of Yahweh in Jesus the Messiah. For South Africans, blackness means Africanness. That is why D. D. L. Makhatini can write: "Black Theology investigates customs and traditions of black people in the light of God's Word,"[86] and Desmond Tutu holds that "Black Theology is an aspect of African Theology. That is to say not all African Theology is Black Theology, but the converse: that all Black Theology . . . is African Theology."[87]

History shows that black people have always believed that Christianity means freedom. Black Theology in its present form proves that black Christians still believe that. This belief has sustained them all along and will continue to do so. Gayraud Wilmore is right: That great black spiritual "O Freedom!" reveals more than anything else what has always been at the heart of black religion:

> O Freedom! O Freedom!
> O Freedom over me!
> And before I'll be a slave,
> I'll be buried in my grave
> And go home to my Lord and be free.

The Black Messiah

We have now come to one of the most central themes in Black Theology: the black theological understanding of Jesus Christ. James Cone observes:

The dialectic of Scripture and tradition in relation to our contemporary social context forces us to affirm that there is no knowledge of Jesus Christ today that contradicts who he was yesterday, i.e., his historical appearance in first-century Palestine. Jesus' past is the clue to his present activity. . . . The historical Jesus is indispensable for a knowledge of the Risen Christ.[88]

This means that Black Theology is not prepared to separate the reality of the historical Jesus from the reality of his presence in the world today. The historical confession of the Christian church that Jesus Christ was "very God and very Man" could only have been based on the testimony of the apostles to the reality of the historical Jesus. Jesus the Christ was not merely godly, but the incarnation of Yahweh, the God who revealed himself to Israel. Yahweh, whom Israel had learned to know "through what he had done" with and for his people, has now made himself known through his Son, through what Jesus, in his turn, was doing with and for people. Thus we understand John 14:9 to read: "To have seen me (act) is to have seen the Father (act)."[89] To understand the acts of Jesus in our history, one must begin to understand his acts while he was on earth. And it is because of this basic truth that Black Theology cannot accept the white Jesus. For, as Vincent Harding writes,

We first met this (white) Christ on slave ships. We heard his name sung in praise while we died in our thousands, chained in stinking holds beneath the decks, locked in with terror and disease and sad memories of our families and homes. When we leaped from the decks to be seized by sharks we saw his name carved in the ship's solid sides. When our women were raped in the cabins, they must have noted the great and holy books on the shelves. Our introduction to this Christ was not propitious and the horrors continued on America's soil.[90]

It is this white Jesus who spoke to blacks in the preaching and lives of white Christians. Always irrevocably on the side of the powerful, he was the guarantee of white *baasskap* and of black subservience and obedience. It was he who blessed the whites' weapons and assured them of victory over Kaffirs and Indians. His gospel, the expectation of the poor, became the blueprint for white law and order, giving the white way of life the sacred glow of divine approval. The exposure of this Jesus is the most significant experience in black Christianity. For black Christians, we affirm with James Cone, to confess Jesus Christ as the Black Messiah is the only true confession of our time.

One of the first black theologians to take the concept of the Black Messiah seriously was Albert Cleage. For him, Jesus was literally black, born to a black woman within the Black Nation of Israel.[91] It seems to us that the literal color of Jesus is irrelevant. As it happens, says James Cone, and we agree with him, he was not white in *any* sense of the word. The importance of the concept of the Black Messiah is that it expresses the concreteness of Christ's continued presence today. Jesus came and lived in this world as the Oppressed One who took upon himself all the suffering and humiliation of all oppressed peoples. As the 1976 Black Theology Statement of the NCBC phrases it:

Black Theology symbolizes Jesus Christ as the Black Messiah to remind black people, in the most forceful manner, that God, through

Christ, takes upon Himself the badge of their suffering, humiliation, and struggle, transforming it by the triumph of his resurrection.[92]

The historical Jesus of the New Testament has a special significance for those who share the black experience. He was poor, the son of poor people who could not bring the prescribed sacrifice at his birth because they could not afford it. Rather, they brought the sacrifice of the poor, two turtledoves instead of the year-old lamb (Lev. 12:6–8, Luke 2:21–24). He belonged to a poor, downtrodden people, oppressed and destitute of rights in their own country and subjugated to countless daily humiliations under the foreign rulers. He lived and worked among the poor and from among these came his disciples. He was one of them, one with them, feeling more at home with the "have nots" than with the "haves." He made no secret of the fact that he had come especially for this kind of people—the poor, the captives, the have-nots, the downtrodden, the kind of people of whom the rich and the affluent and the powerful could speak in the well-known Mammonic jargon:

These people are so uncivilized that the moment they are free, or on their own, they are completely uncontrollable. But if one punishes them regularly and without mercy, one may expect obedience from them and they will serve one well.[93]

As in the Old Testament, the God who comes to us in Jesus the Messiah is the God who takes sides. He is neither indifferent nor aloof. He sides with the poor and the weak, prefers to speak of himself as a "servant," becomes "a friend of publicans and sinners." His own background is that of the much despised *am ha'aretz*—the poor of the land. He is the Oppressed One whose life reflects so much of the life of oppressed people. He was a man without majesty, as Isaiah puts it, a man of sorrows and familiar with suffering. He knew what it was like to live without having a sense of belonging, to be ready to flee for his life at a moment's notice, to be on the alert constantly so as not to fall into the traps of the informers. He lived on earth very much the same way blacks are forced to live. He has made their life his own, he has identified himself with them: He is the Black Messiah.

But still his name is Yoshua, Savior, Liberator. He preached to all who wanted to hear a message of hope and liberation. His life was an example of divine radicality, a profound disturbance of the existing order.[94] He was revolutionary in that he offered an alternative consciousness to the sterile, ideological postures of the Zealots, the Saduccees, and the Pharisees. Mostly, they were regarded as things, these "common" people who thronged to hear Jesus. They had no intrinsic value at all except in as far as they were useful to the Romans and their henchmen. Jesus, however, told them that God loved them. He told them that they were of far greater value than the flowers of the fields and the birds of heaven, even while they knew that even Solomon (even Solomon!) in all his glory was not like one of these.

In a country where the Roman fist was the highest authority, his liberating activity affirmed the infinite worth of human personality. An example: When he is at last alone with the woman accused of adultery, he does not expect her to grovel before him in her gratitude, but he recognizes her womanhood in entrusting responsibility to her: Go and sin no more! This is clearly an example of the totality of Jesus' liberation. He has the power to establish immediately the fullness of his liberating deed. He grants her forgiveness and in doing this, he claims her for his own, making her a child of God (John 8:1–11).

He defended the common people, those with "no name in the street" (Baldwin), against the religious tyranny of high-priests and scribes: The Sabbath is made for man, not man for the Sabbath; the law is servant to humanity. The political tyrant and henchman of the Romans, Herod, he termed a fox; the self-righteous Pharisees he called "white-washed tombs, serpents, brood of vipers" because they "eat up the houses of defenseless widows" while saying long prayers. Like a prophet of old he judges with a terrible harshness, for they "have neglected the weightiest matters of the Torah—justice,

mercy, good faith" (Matt. 23). Wherever Jesus went, he was
the incarnation of the songs of justice in the Psalms:

Yahweh, forever faithful, gives justice to those denied it;
gives food for the hungry, gives liberty to prisoners.
Yahweh restores the sight of the blind,
Yahweh straightens the bent,
Yahweh protects the stranger,
he keeps the orphan and widow (Ps. 146).

It is this Jesus who had died and was resurrected and is truly
present in the community of the oppressed today. To quote
again the 1976 NCBC statement:

Insofar as he is the conqueror of death and all the principalities and
powers, he is the Black Messiah who was raised from the dead to
liberate the oppressed by the power of the God who delivered Israel
from the hand of pharaoh and revealed himself as a Strong Deliverer
and Liberator from every oppression of human existence.

As at the first, he takes it upon himself, and through his Spirit
he discloses his will to restore wholeness to the broken and
fragmented lives of those who trust in him for their liberation.
And as at the first, he shall not fail them.

CHAPTER TWO

The Courage To Be

On Power

Powerlessness breeds a race of beggars.
                    NCNC Statement on Black Power, 1966

*The time when change could be averted in South Africa by
merely reaching for a gun has irrevocably passed.*
                                        Peter Randall

DEFINING POWER

In this chapter we want to examine the phenomenon of power.
In speaking of power, we do not mean what is known as
"powers of the universe," natural forces, or forces of the
cosmos, e.g., floods, drought, or famine. These phenomena
constitute forces, energies one can say, and they only gain the
quality of power when granted that in a sort of mythological
way by people.

The word "power" has an especially negative meaning in
western society. It is, to say the least, a contaminated word.
Jacob Burckhardt's dictum: "Die Macht an sich ist böse," and
Lord Acton's "all power corrupts, and all absolute power
corrupts absolutely" are still largely determinative for the understanding of power.[1] This is partly due to the fact that in
western society power is always acknowledged by the seri-
ousness of the threat, the amount of money, or the destruc-

tiveness of the violence it constitutes or represents. While not
disclaiming the element of truth in this argument, we do not
want to succumb to the temptation of denouncing power as
such and thereby, probably, leaving it to the devil. It is our
purpose to begin by speaking of power as a social, psychological, historical reality.

Power, being a social reality, cannot exist *an sich,* on its own.
John Locke and Bertrand Russell have long since conclusively
argued that power is a relational reality.[2] As such, it has to do
with concrete relations in our socio-historical world. This relational aspect of power is important, for it presupposes that
power has to do with responsive persons, which in turn means
that one cannot say simply that power is "good" or "evil."
Because power has no existence of its own and is at the disposal of people, its strongest characteristic is its ambivalence.

Most modern sociological definitions of power are negative.[3] Power is seen either as the ability to force one's will on
others, or as the ability to confine others to a certain pattern of
behavior. We pause to point out here that these definitions
take as point of departure a concept of power *over others,* which
is essentially an estranged power. Contrasted to that is power
shared *with others,* which means that power is not an alienated
force, but service to others. In the following pages we shall
endeavor to clarify this statement.

Johan Galtung speaks of three types of power over others:
ideological power, remunerative power, and punitive power.[4]
Ideological power is the power of ideas; remunerative power is
the power of the economy; and punitive power is the power to
destroy, force, the power of violence. A society can be struc-
tured in such a way that either one or all of these types of
power are dominant. Less negative, still others speak of power
simply as the ability to achieve purpose.[5] A very good work-
able formula is offered by the definition of P. Thoenes. Power
is, according to him, the concentration of ability.[6] He understands "concentration" as a purposeful, deliberate concentration, and "ability" as the ability to rule, to control, and to
continue to control. It is the ability to create.

This results in the use of means of which Thoenes notes four:

1. Organization: communication, dissemination of information, honoring one's responsibilities and doing one's duties;
2. Energy: the ability to do, being in control of the material one intends to use;
3. Resources: e.g., money;
4. Knowledge: which is connected with the first.

Thus power has to do with the ability to create, to control, to rule, which is to lead. With regard to this we agree with E. Ed. Stern who writes that

> to lead is another kind of service than to follow, but the difference is not a difference in power or domination, for both are service, both are under reciprocal control and authority.[7]

The Courage to Be . . .

We have found the definition of Thoenes to be an acceptable one. More so because it lacks the negativeness of most other definitions and correctly stresses the element of ability which is, in our opinion, indispensable when speaking of power. Where ability lacks, powerlessness abounds. At the same time we must point out a certain vacuum in Thoenes's construction. "Ability to," as used by Thoenes, points to a program, an outward reality, so to speak, but Thoenes neglects the relational aspect of power, which presupposes also an "inward reality." Our point is this. For power as *power over others* to work, some kind of basic submissiveness to the power-wielder is needed.[8] This submissiveness, in its turn, presupposes a certain alienation both vis-à-vis oneself and others. In other words, one must, in some way or another, accept that the other has a right to be submitted to. When this alienation is replaced by identification with oneself, by self-respect and self-affirmation, it can no longer be taken for granted that the ideas of others are superior to one's own, nor that the disparity between the *is* and the *ought* with regard to one's life is "natural" or satisfactory.

The central point in the power-over-others relation is dependency. Substitute for the element of dependency the ability to create one's own resources or the creative use of the resources one has, and the power-over-others pattern is broken. The same happens when the dependent discovers the dependency of the power-wielder on what the other has to offer, e.g., in labor forces. The principle also holds true for the power-over relation based on fear. If one replaces the fear of the violence (the punitive power) of the power-wielder with courage and determination rooted in the self-identification mentioned above, the basis of this particular power-over-others relation is eliminated.[9] But before the external power-over relation can be challenged, this essential inner self-affirmation must be established. This inner reality is that other kind of power Paul Tillich called the "courage to be."[10] The power or courage to be is the basic need to affirm one's own being. It arises from the feeling and the certainty of one's own dignity. Dignity, derived from the Latin *dignus*, meaning "worthy," is a feeling of intrinsic worth, "an essential for every mentally healthy human being" (May). The certainty of this dignity gives one the courage "to be," to self-affirmation. Self-affirmation is not identical, but nonetheless closely related to consciousness—knowing that one is able to, consciously overcoming opposition against the assertion of one's dignity. And in the situations where opposition is overcome, power becomes actualized. The power to be becomes evident in the struggle against what Tillich has called nonbeing. Tillich sees nonbeing as all factors that destroy and negate originality; as hostility, which shrinks courage, generosity, and the capacity to understand the other. Nonbeing also means destructiveness and, eventually, death itself. The aim is not to overlook expressions of nonbeing, but to confront them directly, to accept them as a challenge, endeavor to absorb them—all of which reduces their destructive power. Out of this struggle comes creativity. And being able to create is being able to be human, sharing in God's power of creation.

These two realities, the inner and the outward, do not represent two visions of power. They are complementary to one another, merely two sides of the same coin. The one cannot survive without the other. The inner reality, the identification with one's self, self-affirmation—this is essential and comes first, for it is the indispensable precondition for the quest for human freedom (Freire). But it cannot survive without the other—the outward practical manifestation of this realization. The power to be, the courage to affirm one's human dignity, must inevitably lead to the transformation of structures to fulfil its search for completion and wholeness.

Elucidation

We have now defined our understanding of power, and our argumentation leads us to conclude that there is no reason to hold that power as such is evil. We believe this also for another reason. Power belongs to the very essence of humanity, in the very center of our creaturely relatedness to God. We were created in the "image" and "likeness" of God. Image and likeness are designated by the words *zēlēm* and *demuth*. The term *demuth* does not allude to any kind of physical likeness, but rather describes our unique relation to God. The term *zēlēm* as used in the Old Testament (and also in the *Umwelt*) is not a morphological, but rather a functional, dynamic expression.[11]

According to A. Kruyswijk, this expression conveys that human beings are the image of God by virtue of the divine power granted us by God which works in us. Kruyswijk emphasizes that

what is of importance here is not for man to be regarded as the physical likeness of God. Much more does this likeness express that man, to a certain measure, acts like God.[12]

The whole story of Gen. 1 and 2 is an attempt to give expression to this creaturely relatedness of human beings to God. The responsibility that flows from this relationship is "dominion over creation." This, of course, has not only to do with the source whence this power comes (God), but also with that over which we have been given dominion—the created world, and with those with whom we are to share this unique ability: our fellow human creatures.

In the Bible, the limitations of human power are qualified very clearly. Man is not only reminded of his special relationship to God which makes him "almost a God" (Ps. 8), but he is also reminded where he comes from: He is made of the earth and shall return to the earth (Gen. 1; Ps. 90). The earth shall offer him his livelihood. Moreover, the story of creation itself brings in this subtle nuance. Man receives dominion over the rest of creation while he himself is portrayed as utterly defenseless, without protection, without weapons or the means to assert himself. Seen from this point of view, the expression "dominion" can be understood as having power while being dependent upon. There is a definite element of service incorporated here. There is an interdependence between man and creation. [13]

Because human power is grounded in the power of God, it must reflect the character of the divine power in order to be genuine. God's power is a liberating, creative power, and it is this "full authority" with which God has endowed humanity. To share power and to share in power is to be fully human. It means to be able *to be*, to live in accordance with one's God-given humanity. It means to be able to realize this essential humanity in the socio-historical world in which people have responsibility. Human responsibility presupposes freedom, which is power shared.

To share in power enables human beings to become the subject of their humanity, to assume responsibility, to act responsibly and in acting to realize their own being and that of others. Power, seen as service, as meaningful only in the light of God's gift, can only mean realizing one's humanity as much as God has affirmed it in liberating people to be truly human, in making the world not a chaos, but a place in which to live. Once more: power, in our understanding, is the courage to be, resulting in the freedom to create the possibilities for the realization of full humanity. It finds its ideal form in serving justice.

ENCOUNTER WITH REALITY

Power, we have found, is relational. It functions within given patterns. This also means that power is at the disposal of human beings to use for good or ill. While essentially given by God for the fulfilment of humanity, for service based on God's liberating act for humankind, power can be abused, made an instrument of people's inhumanity to others.

When this happens, according to Guardini, "there is no longer a responsive person to appeal to," because there is no moral appeal possible. [14] A vacuum ensues, for power abused loosens itself from all responsibility toward God and humanity, has no room for *persons,* for their dignity and their responsibility, isolates itself within the anonymity of an organization or an ideal, and more and more seeks its legitimization from ideological argumentation. Invariably, because it begins with the denial of power as a human, inner reality, it tries to suppress the manifestation of power as an outward reality. Just as invariably, this results in intolerance, repression, intimidation, and all kinds of violence. Inevitably it becomes a system, in a certain sense, but only in a certain sense, leading a life of its own. It becomes a structure, relentlessly victimizing, oblivious of all human factors, although human persons are responsible for it and maintain it.

It has taken black people a long time to shed their innocence and to realize what they are really up against. All through history (with a few notable exceptions), when the efforts of blacks toward liberation were frustrated or thwarted, ignored or violently stopped, this was followed by periods of profound astonishment. Somehow, it seems, it was difficult for black people to understand how white people could have done what they had done to blacks. Blacks thought that somehow whites misunderstood, or that the wrong method had been used. Accordingly, they changed their strategy. Either they went cap in hand, or they burned and looted—both out of sheer frustration. We are able to see now, however, that the failure of blacks in many instances should be ascribed to the fact that they made a wrong analysis, not just because of a faulty assessment of the situation, but also because they, instead of analyzing the situation, analyzed white people. This may not be wrong in itself, but it certainly is not enough.

Instead of relying on a realistic appraisal of the situation, blacks have too often sought the causes of their failure to achieve freedom in some kind of special, generalized moral imperfection in white people. Whites, so the argument went, don't keep their promises, or they are selfish "by nature," or they can't help being evil. At best, white people are then regarded as "bad"; at worst, they are "the devil." Albert Cleage is certainly right in saying that white people are not "by nature" worse than any other people. They are just human beings who, for reasons well known, abuse their power. [15]

Toward the end of their lives both Martin Luther King and Malcolm X came to recognize the reality of the white power structure and consequently their analysis and interpretation of the black situation changed and became at once effective. [16] They came to see that it is not really a question of finding a cure for some unspecified moral ailment of whites; it is simply a question of how best to deal with the white power structure. It was this realization which enabled them to get to the heart of the problem, but also it directly caused their violent, untimely deaths.

So this is rather a new experience for blacks. After the elation and the joy, the hope and fatigue, the pain and death, the white power structure in America remains essentially intact. After years of nonviolent struggle and appeals to Christian consciences, with leaders imprisoned or banned, some in exile and some dead, South Africa is still *white* South Africa; white power still runs the country inexorably down its road of violence and destruction. To black people, the "white power structure" offers a good example of power abused.

E. Ed. Stern believes that in situations like the above-mentioned, it is no longer valid to speak of "power" at all. [17] According to Stern, power is a positive reality, meaning that power is not neutral, but "good." Speaking of power where it is being abused, says Stern, is proposing an ethic of power-lessness. The ethical good is always "what is possible." In other words, power is always good; power abused is no power at all, but powerlessness. Power is constituted by obedience to God, according to Stern, i.e., by doing justice. The "power of the world" consists of oppression, injustice, and violence, and the only way to denote such a power is as "pseudopower." Whenever power resorts to violence, it becomes power-lessness. Despite the fact that Stern is not completely clear in his usage of the term "power," it must be said that he has offered most valuable insights. Power in its purest form is indeed obedience to God, who calls for justice and liberation. For Stern, to have true power is never to rule over, but to *share with*, a view we agree with. It is less easy, however, to follow his reasoning when he so easily slips from power to power-lessness to pseudopower. If power abused becomes power-lessness, why use the term "pseudopower" at all? We contend that when power is abused, as blacks daily experience, it does indeed become a powerlessness, but then a *powerlessness of the powerful*. This is a contradiction we should like to emphasize, because it portrays so clearly the fact that the enslaved, having lived a life of contradiction under oppression, in moving to affirm their humanity, have highlighted the enslaved position of the oppressors. It is now they who have to find a way to deal with the contradiction in their lives and this contradiction marks their powerlessness. They are delivered into the au-tonomy of their own power structure, and they are in need of the other. They need the liberation of the oppressed in order to be liberated themselves.

The reality of the matter is that power, even in its demonic form, does exist. It will never do for blacks to determine, with the rather simple joyfulness of Stern, that because this is a power not in accord with the purposes of God, it is power-lessness in the sense that it is no longer there. Blacks have to know that the battle is against a demonic power structure. The powerlessness of those in power will ultimately become man-ifest in its own destruction. In the meantime it is real, charac-terized by injustice and untruth, victimizing those who seek justice. It is up to the powerless to build a power based on righteousness to counter the power of the oppressor. A.J. Rasker has spoken well on this point. He writes:

Our western politics takes on the character of denial of the poor. We feel threatened by them because their legitimate desires endanger *our* system, *our* way of life, *our* egotistical welfare structure. That is why each aspiration for transformation of the existing order is branded communism; why what is to the poor a bridgehead in their march to true freedom is blocked by us and our allies as a dangerous monster . . . , or suppressed by preventative contrarevolutions . . . or simply rooted out with measureless violence. We threaten their form of freedom because they threaten our form of freedom. And for the time being they are still the powerless and we the powerful—as long as it lasts. But in the long run this violence (of ours) will become powerless, because the goal we say we want to reach— justice, freedom, peace—cannot be reached by these means. [18]

All this becomes clear in the power of the powerless who, for the sake of liberation and justice, unmask in their struggle the real nature of the power structure. They also unmask the powerlessness of the powerful in revealing the estranged humanity, the distorted being of the oppressor. The struggle of the oppressed reveals an inner authority which is authentic power because it is born of their desire for justice, liberation, and the wholeness of life.

Because Stern does not clearly distinguish between the different forms of violence, it is rather difficult to follow him in his argumentation that all violence is a sign of powerlessness, so that for Stern the violence of God, described so vividly in the Old Testament, becomes a sign of God's powerlessness. [19] In maintaining that in the resort to violence the true sense of power is lost, Stern undoubtedly expresses a psychological as well as a political truth. Rollo May states that force is the "lowest common denominator of power." [20] He goes on to say, however, that it is utopian to try to divorce power completely from some form of compulsion and coercion. One thinks immediately of the forms of compulsion one has to use in the nonviolent struggle: pressure and confrontation, the process Martin Luther King called "creating tension in the mind."

We must come to some conclusion. It is clear that the temptation surrounding power is so great that it is safe to speak of the ambivalent character of power. This manifests itself clearly in the power-over versus the power-with relation. The same holds true for powerlessness. If power is not a creative force toward liberation, justice, and genuine community, it becomes dehumanized, demonic, self-destructive.

The power of the powerless is the power of truth—the truth about the inhumanity of the oppressor which exposes the lies, injustice, and fear on which the demonic power structure parasitizes in order to survive. This truth is not just to be heard and acknowledged; it is to be believed and done. Black Power is thus the truth about white and black people, about history and the present. This truth opens perspectives for the future and becomes authentic reality in the action of love within history; this truth shall make us free.

THE COURAGE TO BE BLACK: BLACK POWER

The Concept

In the aftermath of the deaths of Malcom X and Martin Luther King, Jr., of the riots and the Black Panthers, Black Power has become a thoroughly obscure concept. Both blacks and whites misunderstood and had misconstrued Black Power to such an extent that even in the minds of black people the confusion is not yet cleared. In this regard valuable work had been done by Carmichael, Hamilton, and Cone, and we can do no more than add some perspectives from the South African point of view.

Black Power is the "answer to the white power structure,"[21] the answer to racism, degradation, humiliation, exploitation, and alienation. Black Power means discovering that the white power structure defines the reality of black life. It means discovering that there is no innocent way of going through life—that innocence is a refusal to face reality, a clinging to empty promises, which makes blacks apathetic. It is learning to discern what really matters, for instance, that the solution does not lie in screaming to white people that they are devils, but in confronting their power with another kind of power.

Black Power realizes that the race problem is essentially a white problem. But at the same time it is also a black problem: The strongest ally of the oppressor is the mind of the oppressed. White power as such is not extraordinary or unusual, it has nothing of the mythological divinity or sacred sanction some whites claim for it, most whites believe in, and all whites enjoy the fruits of. Hamilton and Carmichael have made this clear:

Whenever a number of persons within a society have enjoyed for a considerable period of time certain opportunities for getting wealth, for exercising power and authority, and for successfully claiming prestige and social deference, there is a strong tendency for these people to feel that these benefits are theirs *by right*. [22]

This analysis holds true for the United States as well as for South Africa. If this happens (as it obviously did) within a society where a special significance is attached to the color of one's skin and where color of skin also designates the rich and the poor, the privileged and the under-privileged, racism becomes a reality. And racism, again according to Carmichael and Hamilton, is "the predication of decisions and policies on considerations of race for the purpose of subordinating a racial group and maintaining control over that group." [23] This is the context within which Black Power was born.

The "white power structure," far from being just a term, represents a reality blacks encounter every day. It represents the economic, political, cultural, religious, and psychological forces which confine the realities of black existence. Concretely, for black South Africans the white power structure is manifested in *apartheid*. Whatever grandiloquent ideal this ideology may represent for white people, for blacks it means bad housing, being underpaid, pass laws, influx-control, migrant labor, group areas, resettlement camps, inequality before the law, fear, intimidation, white bosses and black informers, condescension and paternalism; in a word, black powerlessness.

The white power structure represents full control of whites over the instruments of power and over the major resources of the country. It represents an unending spiral of violence inherent in the system of *apartheid*. [24] It is this structure which ensures that the future of black children is as uncertain as the present is for their parents:

We cannot even begin to talk about equality of education in contemporary South Africa. Coming from already disadvantaged home backgrounds, black children have nothing like the well-developed preschool system available to whites. They face additional financial burdens compared to white children, since they must pay school levies and purchase most of their text books, *if* they are fortunate enough to get admitted to a school. Their teachers, who often have to teach double sessions, are generally poorly paid and their classes tend to be almost three times as large in average as those of whites. No wonder there is a high dropout rate, with fully 25 per cent of African children leaving school after their first year, and less than 1 per cent proceeding to the end of secondary school. By the end of Std. 2 more than half the African children admitted in Sub. A will have left to join street gangs, the newspaper vendors, and the crowds of caddies who on occasion had to be controlled with whips and dogs as they clamoured for work. [25]

Blacks realize that *apartheid*, although it has developed into a most formidable system, has no mythical power of its own. It was designed, carefully planned, and is being ruthlessly executed by people—white people. Therefore, it can only be changed by human beings, by people committed to gaining their freedom.

King and Black Power

One of the most profound critics of the Black Power concept was Martin Luther King, Jr. [26] Because King was what he was, it is important to take cognizance of his criticism. King began by making clear that the problem is not the concept of power, or even *Black Power*; it was how this concept was understood that caused the problem. King assessed the cry for Black Power as "a cry of disappointment," born from despair, pain, and hurt. The call for Black Power, he found, is a reaction to the failure of white power. [27]

But all the same, Black Power is the result of white injustice, lethargy, and abuse. It is the result of the inconsistency of the government with regard to violence and racism. Black Power, King recognized, is a call to black people to amass their political and economic strength to achieve their legitimate goals. Power, properly understood, is the ability to achieve purpose.[28] It is the strength required to bring about social, political, or economic changes, and in this sense it is not only desirable but necessary, "in order to implement the demands of love and justice."[29] This brings King to the question of love and power. Love and power are not contrasted. The contrast is imposed only because love is identified with a resignation of power and power with a denial of love. King, however, maintained that

power without love is reckless and abusive and love without power is sentimental and anemic. Power at its best is love implementing the demands of justice. Justice at its best is love correcting everything that stands against love.[30]

King knew that there is, therefore, nothing essentially wrong with power. Already we note this as a most important point of agreement between King and the Black Power advocates. Yet power, he went on to say, may be abused, as has happened in the United States, "and it is precisely this collision of immoral power with powerless morality which constitutes the major crisis of our times."[31] It is, therefore, necessary for blacks to seek to transform their conditions of powerlessness into creative and positive power. King recognized that Black Power is a "psychological call to manhood,"[32] and he spoke of the necessity to change the sense of inferiority that has been instilled in black people through the centuries.[33] Although King was not altogether happy with the (strategic) call to "go it alone," he very explicitly refused to call this, as many who think they echo him do, "black racism":

It is inaccurate to refer to Black Power as racism in reverse, as some have recently done. Racism is a doctrine of the congenital inferiority and worthlessness of a people. . . . The major proponents of Black Power have never contended that the white man is innately worthless.[34]

In spite of the positive aspects, however, King believed that beneath the satisfaction of a gratifying slogan Black Power "is basically a nihilistic philosophy born out of the conviction that the Negro cannot win."[35] Black Power is born out of the belief that American society is so corrupt that change from within is impossible. Black Power, he believed, is a revolution born in despair and without hope, a revolution that was doomed to fail. It merely becomes a catchall for evanescent and futile gestures. The call for a separate black road King regarded as unrealistic. Political strength, especially in a country like the United States, required coalitions. In a multi-racial society all the different groups need each other. King was worried about the exclusion of the white "minority who has fought and will fight against injustice," and he warned blacks against the kind of narrow-mindedness that whites have had.

Yet the most destructive feature of Black Power King found in the call for retaliatory violence. Note that King used the term "retaliatory violence." King asked: how effective is this violence going to be? The argument that blacks in the U.S.A. are "part of the Third World" and could therefore expect help from that side he regarded as "beyond the realm of serious discussion."[36] He pointed out that violence is futile in the struggle for justice, a fact proven by the riots, which did not bring any tangible results. Moreover, violence undermines the ability to appeal to the white conscience. Its ultimate weakness, however, is that violence is a descending spiral, begetting the very thing it seeks to destroy:

Through violence you may murder the liar, but you cannot murder the lie, nor establish the truth. . . . Returning violence for violence multiplies violence, adding deeper darkness to a night already devoid of stars.[37]

King understood that through Black Power blacks seek a new society, a new way of living, an alternative for the violence, injustice, and oppression under which they are now forced to live. This is precisely why he could not understand the call for retaliatory violence:

One of the greatest paradoxes of the Black Power movement is that it talks unceasingly about not imitating the values of white society, but in advocating violence it is imitating the worst, the most brutal, and the most uncivilized value of American life.[38]

King Criticized

One of the most adequate responses to King's criticism of Black Power was given by Joseph Washington.[39] King's view that Black Power is born out of despair, Washington says, is inseparably linked to the issue of violence. Whereas King believed that Black Power's call for violence means the conviction that blacks can't win, Washington states boldly: "*nonviolence* is a no-win policy. Whatever else may be said, Black Power is born of the conviction that violence is the only win policy."[40]

King was convinced that violence "can't work." Washington disputes this and argues that King is unable to distinguish between a rebellion and a revolution. King should not overlook the fact that the slave revolts had not really gained the support of the masses. The case may be totally different today. Where the slave insurrections lacked planning, organization, and fire-power, this need not be so today. "The revolution Black Power intends as violence is to bring the nation to a halt and turn it around."[41] The real issue is one of time, for it may well be that Black Power is an idea whose time has not yet come.[42] Washington denies that the only way to appeal to white consciences is through nonviolence. Violence is no less an appeal:

This time, however, white consciences will be formed in the crippling of America's economic development, the destruction of her property, the death of thousands of whites, and perhaps, the extermination of millions of blacks. Black Power really believes that only through "dis mess" will white consciences cry out: Oh, Lawd, I'm tired a dis mess![43]

According to Washington, violence is the only way through which a better America can be created. He is not impressed by King's argument that violence only begets violence, and hate, hate. Nonviolence only begets nonviolence, and the movement is stopped dead in its tracks:

Hate we will have with us always. But Black Power has a vision of a society where hate will not take the form of racism. It concludes that we must get the race hate out of our system once and for all; the cleanest and the quickest way of doing so is through violence.[44]

Washington saw clearly that the disagreement with King is not over power, for that is what King has always sought through nonviolence. The real issue is violence. Washington argues that King, of all people, could not reproach Black Power advocates that the price of violence will be "casualties by the thousands." It was this very King who had taught blacks that in the nonviolent struggle one should be prepared for casualties by the thousands! The question, Washington concludes, is not one of violence or nonviolence, as King suggests. Rather it is merely one of quality.[45] King was also a militant who desired to change society, to rid it of racial injustice. In their militancy, Black Power advocates intend no less. Washington suggests:

Perhaps Dr. King was such a keen critic of Black Power because he recognized in it the seeds of his own thought come to fruition. . . . He resisted it to the end, but it had an increasing effect on him.[46]

Once More: Black Power

Against the background of our discussion on power in general, we now have three views on Black Power specifically. Before coming to our conclusion, we will examine three important aspects of Black Power.

BLACK POWER IN HISTORY.   Like Black Theology, Black Power as a concept (for that matter, as a movement—Garvey!) is not new. It is as old as creation. Although the struggle for black liberation did not always bring tangible political gain, it had an inner authority, a power beyond words (Buthelezi), bearing suffering with dignity and hope, affirming what is more than merely human. In this sense, Black Power is as old as Black Theology and as such it has always had a close relation with Black Theology—a relation which we will examine in the next chapter.

Throughout history, many blacks have for various reasons accepted white domination. They have played along with the white power structure, again for various reasons. While one must accept the fact that power, in the sense of a concentration of ability to create new structures, to share in the control of those structures, has not been achieved, it is true that inasmuch as the struggle for liberation was waged, Black Power was there.

This is not intended to be a simple judgment on black history. What is important, however, is that there was a struggle through which a basis was created upon which this generation, blessed with new insights and new possibilities, may build. Every single protest through the years of slavery, though in itself not powerful enough to have changed the situation, was an expression of Black Power in that it affirmed, time and again, the desire for freedom and true humanity. When David Walker made his famous statement on slavery it was Black Power expressed:

Fear not the number and the education of our enemies, against whom we shall have to contend for our lawful right, guaranteed to us by our Maker; for why should you be afraid, when God is, and will continue to be (if we continue humble) on our side?[47]

Black Power found expression in Henry Garnett's step-by-step plan for resistance;[48] in Frederick Douglass's reminder to blacks that "there is no progress without struggle;"[49] in Marcus Garvey's "Back to Africa Movement." It found expression in Enoch Mgijima's struggle when he and his people preferred to die rather than give up the freedom they had found in the Bullhoek community;[50] in Chief Gonnema and his Hottentot people when they fought their hopeless war against the colonists in the Cape, trying to regain their cattle and their land and with it their dignity as a people.[51] Black people must come to respect this proud tradition, a tradition which produced Kimpa Vita, the African prophetess who was burned to death for preaching the Black Messiah in the Congo of the eighteenth century; a tradition which produced Albert Luthuli, Malcolm X, and Martin Luther King, Jr. And it is in this tradition that Onkgopotse Tiro stood when he ended his famous speech at the University of the North in 1973:

In conclusion, Mr. Chancellor, I say: Let the Lord be praised, for the day shall come when all men shall be free to breathe the air of freedom which is theirs to breathe. And when that day shall have come, no man, no matter how many tankers he has, will reverse the course of events.[52]

BLACK POWER: THE IMPLICATIONS.   When one embraces Black Power as a concept, one automatically becomes involved in Black Power as a movement. In other words, Black Power very definitely has implications—on the personal as well as on the socio-political levels. To begin with, the implications of Black Power are psychological. We have argued that power begins with the essential identification with oneself, with a positive self-affirmation. One becomes aware of one's position, of one's identity and the need to challenge the ideological power of the oppressor.

One discovers that it is always the oppressors who have the right to define both history and the present situation of people. They define the identity of the oppressed, which in a situation of oppression usually also defines their social position, so that, within the South African context, the label "coloured," which really means nothing at all, comes to mean "someone who is evidently not white" and, therefore, inferior. This last consequence is confirmed by the laws which apply to this category of people. The same happens when one is designated as a "Bantu."

Because the oppressors also control the instruments which regulate the way of life of the oppressed (parliament for example), their position allows them, ultimately, to lead the thinking of the oppressed into patterns of thought designed for them. But Black Power holds that black people should have the right to interpret both history and the present situation in their own terms.

Perhaps the most appropriate description of this process of self-identification is the concept of Black Consciousness. That is why we have spoken of Black Consciousness as an integral part of Black Power. It means cognizance of the fact that at present the social, political, and economic status of black people is determined by the color of their skin and its connotations in white society. That is why Martin Luther King was correct when he wrote:

Black Power is a psychological reaction to the psychological indoctrination of the perfect slave. . . . One must not overlook the positive value in calling the Negro to a new sense of manhood, to a deep feeling of radical pride and to an audacious appreciation of his heritage. The Negro must be grasped by a new realization of his dignity and his worth. He must stand up amidst a system that still oppresses him and develop an unassailable and majestic sense of his own value. He must no longer be ashamed of being black.[53]

Because this Black Consciousness does not primarily designate color of skin, it enables black people to form new alliances on a basis completely foreign to the oppressors' way of thinking and thereby effectively divests them of their ideological power over blacks.

Black Power's implications for the church begin with a reinterpretation of church history and a reconsideration of the role of missions and missionaries. Though no one will deny the important and sometimes even liberating role missionaries have played in the history of black people, we must be very honest in ascertaining precisely to what extent the missionary movement had participated (and is participating) in the oppression of black people. In other words, the test becomes this: Is missionary enterprise an expression of service toward liberation, or an expression of oppressive power? An evaluation of the prophetic witness of the church with regard to socio-political questions in the light of the black situation establishes the link between Black Theology and Black Power.

In the socio-political field Black Consciousness and Black Power imply that whites can no longer play the role they have played traditionally with regard to "black politics." This means that blacks must do their own thing and that whites, "conservatives" as well as "liberals," can no longer make a decisive contribution. As far as we are concerned, there is only room for those whites who share so deeply the concern of black people that they are willing to work for the radical change of oppressive societal structures wherever this is needed.

In South Africa the situation is such that political integration, in other words, black/white coalitions, cannot be realistically discussed. On these grounds alone, the cry of racism in reverse is nonsensical. For both the United States and South Africa, Carmichael and Hamilton have spoken well on this point. They observe:

This is a deliberate and absurd lie. There is no analogy—by any stretch of the definition or the imagination—between the advocates of Black Power and white racists. Racism is not merely exclusion on the basis of race but exclusion for the purpose of subjugating or maintaining subjugation. . . . The black people [of America] have not lynched whites, bombed their churches, murdered their children and manipulated laws and institutions to maintain oppression. White racists have.[54]

The argument speaks for itself.

BLACK POWER: THE MEANS.   Although this point will be discussed again in chapter 5, a few remarks are appropriate here. Black Power enables black people to determine by what means they will reach their goals. This does not mean that the discussion begins and ends with the issue of violence. It does mean, however, that blacks should have the right to determine whether nonviolence is the only possible philosophy blacks should adhere to, or, conversely, that violence is the only possible form of expression left for blacks.

Washington, we have seen, pleads for violence as the "only win policy," as the essential expression of Black Power. Carmichael and Hamilton hold that violence is necessary for self-defense, that it is essential for black self-respect:

Each time the black people [in the cities in the North] saw Dr. Martin Luther King get slapped, they got angry. When they saw little black girls bombed to death *in a church* and civil rights workers ambushed and murdered, they were angrier; and when nothing happened, they were steaming mad. We had nothing to offer that they could see, except to go out and be beaten again.[55]

In the same vein, James Baldwin had earlier expressed his belief when he wrote that neither civilized reason nor Christian love would cause white people to treat a black as they themselves presumably wanted to be treated. "Only the fear of your power to retaliate would cause them to do that. . . . "[56] Retaliatory violence is necessary for the affirmation, the self-respect, the manhood of black people. This is reminiscent of the Black Muslim slogan:

Fight like hell with those who fight like hell against you, and the world of mankind will respect you as equals.[57]

Even more profound than the issue of violence, another, deeper matter is at stake here. In the choice for the new black image, blacks are making a choice for a new existence, a new way of living. We have seen enough of white racism, said Adam Small; blacks *cannot* be racist in their blackness. Should this same principle apply to matters like violence as well? Is the right to strike back essential to the black person's self-esteem? With that we are faced once more with the question of Martin Luther King and with that of Vincent Harding, which also becomes ours:

The basic human search for a definition of manhood is here set out in significant black lineaments. Does manhood indeed depend upon the capacity to defend one's life? Is this American shibboleth really the source of freedom for men? Is it possible that a man simply becomes a slave to another man's initiative when he feels obliged to answer the opponent on the opponent's terms? Is there perhaps a certain kind of bondage involved when men are so anxious about keeping themselves alive that they are ready to take the lives of others to prevent that occurrence? The question is really one of the image man was meant to reflect; what is it?[58]

Indeed, what is the new black image, the true human image, blacks are meant to reflect? If what one does is so closely linked to what one was *meant to be*, is there such a thing as the *right* to use violence? These are clearly questions only black people have the right to ask. Whites have lost that right, except those few who live like Beyers Naudé. But these are also questions black people must honestly grapple with if they are to enjoy authentic liberation. Black Power's concern is the essential humanity of black people. Its concern is self-affirmation, self-respect, pride, participation in and control of the black's own human destiny. It says "Yes" and "No." Indeed, but "Yes" and "No" *to what?* It is in this choice that the fulfilment of black authenticity lies.

CONCLUSIONS.   In making our final conclusion, we go back to the views of King and Washington. Washington is right; the real point of disagreement is not power, but violence and nonviolence. That King could speak of power, but had trouble with the stress on *black* power, must be understood in the light of his convictions on integration. Washington is also right in disputing that Black Power is born "out of despair."

It is ironic that King should have thought that this despair, and therefore Black Power, is the result of the failure *(sic!)* of white power. Rather, it is the awareness of the very existence—which King concedes—and indeed, the *success* of white power that made Black Power, in King's words, "not only desirable, but necessary." If whites had known that power, in order to be authentic, has to be shared and not used as an instrument to exploit and oppress, it would not have been necessary for black people to create their own power base. Now they have to—to meet the oppression of the white power structure. Far from being a cry of hopelessness and disappointment, Black Power is a clear, cool-minded realization of the cultural, political, and economic reality of contemporary society, a society in which white power calls the tune.

One must realize, however, that this was not Martin Luther King's last word. Toward the end of his life King underwent some significant changes on almost all important matters. He became more critical of American society and would no longer be satisfied with small changes "within this system." He also saw more clearly that the struggle in America was not so much a struggle of the "cosmic forces" of good versus evil, but a decidedly human struggle against a demonic white power structure, a struggle in which the poor of the earth are involved.[59] Washington is right when he says that King's role in preparing the way for Black Power and Black Consciousness must not be underrated. But Washington errs when he concludes that the difference between King and himself is not violence or nonviolence, but "merely" one of quality. It is not "merely" a question of quality, it is *precisely* one of quality!

For Martin King, nonviolence was, to the very end, more than a mere practicality; it was a life's conviction. Even though he could understand that people will turn to violent measures when all else fails and he himself never made an "eternal principle" out of nonviolence,[60] this is not to say that he condoned it. Indeed, King was a militant who never denied the necessity for tension, conflict, and confrontation. But to him, conflict and confrontation were never "on their own" ends in themselves. He never used them as the antithesis of love so that even within the conflict situation confrontation was a vehicle toward reconciliation. This constitutes a difference of some significance.

One may conclude from Washington's argumentation that for him too violence is the "only way out." King, on the other hand, made it palpably clear that he was not impressed with this "practical" way out that people have followed for so long. "Solving problems with violence" he said, "has led the world inexorably to deeper confusion and chaos."[61]

King was convinced that history now needs people who dare to break away from the violent past to create new possibilities for a new future. In this, Martin King spoke not only to blacks, but to all people:

Humanity is waiting for something other than blind imitation of the past. If we want truly to advance a step further, if we want to turn over a new leaf and really set a new man afoot, we must begin to turn mankind away from the long and desolate night of violence.[62]

We submit that this argumentation carries a lot more weight than Washington's shortsighted violent ethic. Washington's reasoning does not eliminate the fact that violence does beget violence and hate an ever new spiral of hatred and violence. His understanding of people and the nature of violence lacks depth if he holds unreservedly to his premise that a violent revolution, in which "thousands of whites and perhaps millions of blacks" will be killed, is the "quickest and cleanest" way to end racial hatred and effect reconciliation.

It is clear that in Washington's thinking power comes out of the barrel of a gun and this is, we have argued above, a falsification of authentic power. Nowhere does Washington seem to take into account that violence, once unleashed, acquires an autonomy of its own of which the inseparable twin is escalation. Whereas Washington does not seem to care about hatred ever deepening, nor about the escalation of inhumanity through more and more violence, we do care. All in all, Washington's thinking is so strongly reminiscent of the ideology of the ruling class that we cannot but reject it outright.

Whereas we do not deny that a situation may arise where retaliatory violence is forced upon the oppressed and no other avenue is left open to them, we do so with a clear hesitancy, knowing full well that it will probably prove a poor "solution" and that violence can never be "justified." Furthermore, the questions of King and Harding haunt us still. Behind these questions lies the deeply disturbing theological question for any Christian, namely this: Is it not the essence of discipleship that the Christian is required to react on a completely different level in order to create and keep open the possibilities for reconciliation, redemption, and community?

If Christians do not take this seriously, Bonhoeffer warns, they will be caught in the quicksand of abstractions and insoluble conflicts. In every situation this decision will have to be made anew, for the activity of Christians is not based merely on the fruits of human wisdom, nor on a separation of "human autonomous ethics" and the "ethic of Jesus." It is born, rather,

out of the joy over the accomplished reconciliation of the world with God, out of the peace effected by the accomplished work of salvation in Jesus Christ, out of the fullness of the all-encompassing life that is Jesus Christ. [63]

This is the source of the action of Christians in the world and this is the conviction on which the action of black people to transform the world should be based.

"Black Power" is, in conclusion, a slogan for the continuous historical effort of black people, writes Gayraud Wilmore, to use resources of culture, politics, and economics to force upon white people a change in existing structures that have not been affected by mere moral suasion and appeals to conscience. It is action to achieve justice and liberation for black people. It does not purport to be the gospel of Jesus Christ, the Holy Spirit, or the true Christian church. Black Theology is *how* black theologians understand Jesus Christ, the Spirit, the church, etc., in relation to justice and liberation; and the praxis, or strategic aspect, of this understanding leads inevitably to the mobilization of black people for participation with *power* in the public arenas of policy and decison-making. [64]

CHAPTER THREE

Where the Spirit Moves . . .

Black Theology and Black Power

If I had-a my way,
If I had-a my way, little children,
If I had-a my way,
I'd a tear this building down.

Black Spiritual

I want to be short and simple. If God is the Creator of heaven and
earth, and if He is the Father of Jesus Christ, and if Jesus Christ
is the Founder of the Church, why should the Church be silent
and do nothing in the face of racism, exploitation and violence,
when these are committed in God's world? Alternatively,
should God withdraw from the history of this world, hand it
over to the devils and restrict Himself to the temples and church
buildings?

Zephania Kameeta

The Holy Spirit is the revolutionary power which comes to an
exploited people as they struggle to escape from powerlessness
and to end the institutional oppression forced upon them by an
enemy, . . . and in our kind of world the language of the Holy
Spirit cannot but be the language of revolt.

Albert Cleage

THE SPIRIT IS THE MOVEMENT

James Cone was the first black theologian who took Black
Power seriously theologically, and in his first book, *Black The-*

ology and Black Power, he endeavored to provide a theological justification for Black Power. Although Cone never explicitly says that Black Power *is* the gospel, he does come perilously close to identifying the two.[1] Black Power is, says Cone, complete emancipation of black people from white oppression by whatever means necessary.[2] Black Power says "no" to oppression and "yes" to the dignity and worth of black people.

Cone also sees Black Power as "the courage to be," the black person's attempt to affirm his being, to be recognized as a *Thou* instead of an *It.* Black Power says that blacks prefer to die rather than live as slaves, for "to be human is to find something worth dying for. When the black man rebels at the risk of death, he forces white society to look at him, to recognize him, to take his being into account, to admit that he *is.*"[3] Black Power is an attitude, an inward affirmation of the essential worth of blackness. To understand what God is doing in the world, according to Cone, one has to know what Black Power is doing, for Black Power, even in its most radical expression, is not the antithesis of Christianity, but rather God's central message to twentieth-century America.[4] "Black rebellion," Cone affirms, "is a manifestation of God Himself involved in the present-day affairs of men for the purpose of liberating a people."[5]

If, Cone argues, the message of Christ frees a man to be for those who labor and are heavily laden, the humiliated and abused, then "it would seem that for twentieth-century America the message of Black Power is the message of Christ Himself."[6] Christianity is not alien to Black Power, and the ghetto rebellions are God's work.[7] For freedom Christ has set you free, Paul wrote to the Galatians. And Cone says: as long as a man is a slave to another power, he is not free to become what he is—human. Thus Black Power has in common with Christianity the liberation of people. Here the formulation of Cone is more careful: "There must be some correlation between Black Power and Christianity,"[8] and again: "It would seem that Black Power and Christianity have this in common: the liberation of man."[9]

The activity of God in the world, Cone goes on to say, is

described in terms of the work of the Holy Spirit working in the lives of people. When one is filled with the Holy Spirit, one becomes completely new, compelled to take sides with the sufferers. The Spirit is the power of Christ himself at work in the life of the believer;[10] it is the power of God, for it means a continuation of God's work for which Christ died.[11] God acts through his Spirit and Black Power is God's new way of acting in America.[12]

God's revelation is black, and the forces of Black Power, to the extent that they are genuinely concerned and seek to meet the need of the oppressed, represent the work of God's Spirit.[13] This formulation is followed immediately by another: "If Christ is present today actively risking all for the freedom of man, *he must be acting through the most radical elements of Black Power.*"[14] For Cone, Black Power is the spirit of Christ himself;[15] it is God's way of saying to blacks that they are human beings and it is God's way of saying to whites: "Get used to it!"[16]

Joseph R. Washington offers his particular view on our subject in his book *Black and White Power Subreption.*[17] For Washington, Black Theology is either the theology of the black revolution or it is no *black* theology at all; just as Black Power is either a "flash in the pan" or a violent revolution.[18] Washington wants a radical theology of revolution which questions the basic structures of society and desires a new political, economic, and social order. This is a demand for justice which essentially means disorder and the creation of a new order. As we have seen in the previous chapter, Washington believes that the only way that this new order would come is through unlimited violence, through "blood full of courage," writing a "bloody peace in the sky."[19]

Black theologians, according to Washington, have not yet called for such a revolution. The revolution does not go far enough. Black theologians, in this regard,

continue to be Martin Luther King's children. They are not Uncle Tom's children by any stretch of the imagination, but neither are they Malcolm X's children.[20]

According to Washington, a realistic appraisal of the situation will reveal that a violent revolution is necessary for the creation of real peace and freedom for both black and white. A theology of revolution, whereby Washington really means a theological justification of a violent revolution, will find its point of departure in the Cross of Jesus:

It is the Cross which reveals war and revolution as the life-giving means to counter-act the misuse of freedom by men with absolute power who tend to use it irresponsibly to abridge the freedom of the powerless. . . . The Cross declares that a just war is as much a risk as an unjust peace, but no more so.[21]

Black Power dreams of a new world, a new order, "an open society in which all men share and find their contribution acceptable and accepted."[22] Just as for Cone, the crucial question for Washington is: What is God doing in the world? The reply is similar: God works through Black Power proclaiming that in order to create a new system, our own systems must first die.[23] The price of liberation and peace which will come in the end is "violence in full force," giving a call for the new earth:

Violence is the only way to power for good. Every and any means is justified; if the end does not justify the means, nothing does.[24]

In the publications so far, South African black theologians hardly speak about Black Power. If they do, it seems mostly in a negative sense. Yet, when one reads carefully, one finds that with some the term Black Consciousness is interpreted in such a way that it really becomes identified with Black Power.[25] So we find the interpretation that Black Consciousness means that blacks must reject all systems that seek to make them foreign in the country of their birth. It means a search for new values. Black Consciousness simultaneously means a "new vision of African tradition" *and* "an awareness of the power blacks wield as a group both economically and politically."[26] In this interpretation, Black Theology is "an extension of Black

Consciousness," a "reflection in the light of our daily experience."[27]

Although the term Black Power is not used, these theologians interpret Black Consciousness as Black Power, and they establish a definite relation between Black Theology and Black Power. This becomes even more clear in the theology of Simon Maimela.[28] He believes that Black Theology has the task of stressing that black people are meant to be free and that this thought must be kept alive in the hearts of those who are engaged in the struggle for liberation. This liberation is God's situational work for black people. Whatever is demanded by the struggle, therefore, is just, for it is a means through which God effects liberation.[29]

Blacks may participate in the struggle without any reservation, knowing they are doing the will of God, i.e., liberating people.[30] Black Consciousness, Maimela writes, is the human responsibility given to people by God (Gen. 1:28), a responsibility to affirm themselves and to make decisions about their own future. Blacks should therefore not be oppressed as a people, but shall rule the earth:

Every earlier attempt as well as the new consciousness and self-affirmation whose purpose is the liberation of blacks must be interpreted by Black Theology as the work of God. . . . Black Theology rejects every understanding of God which does not include *God's full and unreserved identification with the purposes of black people.*[31]

There is a close and conspicuous affinity between the theology of Maimela and that of Albert Cleage, pastor of the Shrine of the Black Madonna. Cleage holds black people to be God's chosen people, the chosen Black Nation. Anything at all that serves the black revolution is the will of God. For Cleage, "that's the only yardstick there is."[32] The will of God is for blacks to be men, to stand up and fight for the things that are theirs:

If anything supports the black liberation struggle, it is good, it is the will of God. Anything that works against this struggle is satanic.[33]

We shall devote a separate discussion to Cleage in the next chapter. For now it is enough to note that Cleage, more than any other black theologian, confesses and brings into practice the complete identification of the gospel with a nationalistic Black Power ideology.

A BLACK POWER RELIGION?

The term "Black Power religion" was used for the first time by Vincent Harding, expressing his concern about the vulnerability of Black Theology merely becoming the handmaid for and finding its framework in the Black Power political program.[34] In this, Harding voices the concern of more black theologians to whose views we shall turn in this part of the discussion.

J. Deotis Roberts used the same term when he discussed Cone's theology expounded in *Black Theology and Black Power*. Roberts has no use for the "narrowness" Cone has imposed on Black Theology[35] and argues for a theology with both liberation and reconciliation as its goal, instead of a theology which may become, as can be seen clearly in the theology of Albert Cleage, a mere religion of Black Power.[36] This is not to say, though, that Roberts rejects Black Power, or the relation between Black Theology and Black Power. According to him, Black Theology is addressed to a powerless people, a people seeking Black Power as a means of liberation from the oppressive control of white power.[37] Roberts speaks, like Cone, of the God of the Bible as the God of the Exodus, of the exile, of the prophets of social justice and as the God of Jesus. "God is not merely present, but he is present *in power*."[38]

This God, Roberts states, is concerned about the total plight of black people, but it is necessary to differentiate between "the religion of Black Power" and Black Theology. The first seeks to be a theological justification for the political, ideological, pseudoreligious elements of black nationalism; the second is the confession of faith in the God who is concerned about blacks.[39]

The Black Power concept Roberts supports cannot be the

same as that of Washington or Cleage. Roberts seeks a Black Power that can be "fully supported by Christian ethics," the kind that "liberates the black man while it leaves the way open for reconciliation between black and white."[40] In his latest book Roberts is even more explicit about the relationship of Black Theology to Black Power. In a chapter entitled: "The Gospel of Power," he writes that this gospel is a gospel of radical involvement in the liberation of the oppressed. It is a gospel of social and political action that will usher in a new human order:

The real question is whether the gospel of Jesus Christ is like aspirin or like dynamite, whether it is a gospel of pacification or a gospel for revolution, whether it is a gospel of the *status quo* and the Establishment or a power for the liberation of the oppressed.[41]

From the South African side, Manas Buthelezi has rejected outright an interpretation which links Black Theology to Black Power, or so it seems. He regards "an indiscriminate alignment of Christian black awareness with an emotionally charged political concept unfortunate."[42] Buthelezi observes:

To interpret the quest for a Black Theology purely in terms of the awakening of black nationalism or the consolidation of Black Power forces is to trifle with one of the most fundamental issues in modern Christianity.[43]

Ernest Baartman, another South African, has this to say: Black Consciousness is the answer to the white gospel. For blacks, this means that they now receive the power to become children of God. Whites who judge Black Theology must know that blacks are not really interested in their criteria, in whether they understand or don't understand Black Theology.[44] Black Consciousness, Baartman goes on to say, is not the same as Black Power, for Black Power implies the use of violence.[45] Blacks, seeing what violence has done to whites, wish to have no part of that.

This does not mean, however, that black people will *never* use violence.[46]

Black Consciousness is a search for power for blacks, but, Baartman concludes, one must begin with an inner power, namely the love of God and the power which is the gift of this love. Blacks must begin with love for themselves, which must enable them to love their white neighbor. It is this love which must convince whites, according to Baartman, to share power with blacks. The power Black Consciousness receives from God is the power of love.[47]

These views of Buthelezi and Baartman have been used by some white theologians to prove the "disparity" between the American and South African expressions of Black Theology as if there were two "theologies."[48] By the same token these theologians have tried to prove that Black Power is foreign to South African black theological thought. It is necessary that we take a closer look at what has been said.

The dictum of Buthelezi stems from 1972. In that same year, he delivered a series of lectures at the University of Heidelberg, Germany, in which he maintained that man, created in the image of God, has a "delegated authority over the creation of God." Man's special relation to God gives him a special status which is linked to the wielding of power.[49] In contrast to this, Buthelezi continues, the black man's experience of life is that of powerlessness, which causes an infringement of black humanity.

To be denied the sharing of power means to be effectively reduced to the level of subhumanity. . . . Any discussion about the humanization of life which excludes the dynamics of power is a fruitless theoretical exercise.[50]

In this sense Buthelezi speaks of the black person's humanity as a "colonized humanity."[51] Thus, to be truly human, one must have power. To be human is to have dominion over the created self; otherwise the created self becomes a caricature. To destroy the caricature and search for true and authentic humanity is human liberation. How, Buthelezi asks, can I have the power to be, that is, dominion over my black self?[52]

It cannot be denied that Buthelezi is speaking of power within a theological context. With this in mind we must assume that his reaction to Black Power must be the result of a misunderstanding. If he warns against a Black Power/Black Theology relationship which is understood purely in terms of black nationalism—a sense in which the operative word seems to be "purely"—or in terms of wanton violence, he is doubtless correct. In our view, however, Buthelezi's rejection of Black Power as a legitimate theological concept is inconsistent with the point of view expressed in his Heidelberg lectures.

Baartman is no less intriguing. Let us begin by establishing that he, like Buthelezi and others, does speak about power. Again we must conclude that Baartman's problem is with a specific interpretation of Black Power and with the Black Theology/Black Power relationship. For what does Baartman say? Black Consciousness is a search for power for blacks. What is the difference between "power for blacks" and "Black Power"? Baartman speaks of the "power of love," which must "convince whites to share power with blacks." What does this mean? What kind of power can whites in South Africa share with blacks except political and economic power?

And what form will the power of love take within the South African context? Baartman gives us further indication in an article he had written on "The Black Man and the Church."[53] In that article he objects to the "monopoly of power by the whites," not only in the political sphere, but also in the church! Blacks, he said, do want power, but they want more "than just power"—they want human beingness, the ability to be, the ability to love, to be a neighbor. In other words, Baartman is pleading for Black Power in terms of our definition, power expressed in self-identification and self-affirmation, a power which seeks the transformation of societal structures to accommodate the new humanity.

GOD IN HISTORY

Our deliberations on Black Theology and Black Power lead us to yet another cardinal matter. We have seen this crop up again and again: the question, namely, of where God is at work in history. *That* God is at work is agreed. The question is only: Where? And how?

This issue is by no means new. The profound theological importance of this matter was strongly emphasized in the theology of M. M. Thomas, that remarkable layman, director of the Christian Institute of Bangalore, India.[54] In 1961, Thomas presented an address to the W.C.C. Assembly in New Delhi, which touched off a long and serious ecumenical discussion.[55] In his address, Thomas stated as his concern the "Christian understanding of the revolution in Asia and Africa today." He took his point of departure from the theme of the Lordship of Christ.

Christ as Lord of history, says Thomas, is at work today in all nations of the world in spite of, and indeed through, the ambiguous political, economic, and social actions in any given country. The upheavals and revolutions, insofar as they represent the search for the "new humanity," for freedom and a new dimension of human life, fulfil the promises of Christ and must be seen as commensurate with the work of God in Christ.

Speaking of God's action within the social changes of our time does not mean that these revolutions determine God's work. No, says Thomas, it is rather the reverse:

that He is in control of the revolutions of history; not that the divine power remains subordinate to the revolutionary purposes of man but that the pressures of God are at work in them and that even the rebellion of man cannot go outside His ultimate purpose and that His power is available for the judgment and renewal of every situation.[56]

Secondly, Thomas is of the opinion that the kingdom of God cannot be identified totally with the church. The church and the world both center around Jesus Christ. Thomas believes that the community of the faith is more than the empirical church, and he seriously questions the division of history into a secular and salvation history. Christians can see, through faith, that the promises of Christ are fulfilled in revolutionary action. "Under the creative providence of God," Thomas writes, "the revolutionary ferment in Africa and Asia has within it the promise of Christ for a fuller and richer life for man and society."[57] These promises of Christ include the new discovery of selfhood, freedom, new forms for society and the search for the meaning of life.

Thirdly, faith can discern the work of Christ in contemporary history. This ability to discern, Thomas argues, "is the basis of Christian spiritual discrimination and Christian ethical responsibility in secular life."[58] Thomas ended with what he called "the three most important rediscoveries" for the churches in Asia and Africa:

1. that the gospel of Jesus Christ should not be identified with any one culture, political order, social ideology or moral system. As the word and deed of God, transcending all cultures, it is the divine power for their judgment and redemption. This is an understanding which gives the Church the ability to relate itself positively but critically to all the creative movements of renewal of man and his world without absolutizing any of them.

2. that the redemption which Jesus Christ offers is the redemption of the world. No doubt the world refers primarily to the world of persons; but the world of persons is involved in the processes of nature, society and history and cannot be considered or saved in isolation. Therefore Christ's judgment and redemption is "social and cosmic" and includes within its scope the world of science and technology, of politics, society and culture, of secular ideologies and religions. The Christian hope guaranteed by the Resurrection of Christ is that all things will be summed up in Him in the end.

3. that Christ is present and active in the world of today, engaged in a continued dialogue with men and nations, affirming his kingly rule over them through the power of His law and His love. The history of His deeds between His resurrection and His coming again in glory holds all other histories within its context and control. So the mission of the Church is not to save itself from the revolutions of our time, but to discern the promise and judgment of Christ in them and to witness to His Kingdom in them, waiting for the day of its final consummation.[59]

Karl-Heinz DeJung correctly pointed out two most significant theological premises which are basic to Thomas's argumentation regarding God's action in history: The first was a desire to determine, amidst the demands of imperialism, communism, and nationalism, the proper place of the Christian church in Asia. The second was a desire to challenge and confront the theological premises of the western churches which had made the humanization of recent Asian history impossible: (a) by holding onto a pietistic missionary theology still dominant in Asian churches; (b) by identification of the European process of civilization with the salvation acts of Christ, seen most clearly in liberal missionary theology; (c) by interpreting the revolutionary processes in Africa and Asia as a desertion of the faith, a denial of the acts of God in Christ—a tendency most evident within European ecumenical theology, faced with crises in Europe itself.[60] For Thomas it was clear that a church which restricts the acts of God in history only to itself cannot avoid the idolization of the world.[61]

What Thomas was saying was this. Through the centuries the churches have often sided with the oppressors in the name of law and order. The question now is whether the churches shall repeat the mistakes of the past, or would they at last begin to preach the gospel as it relates to the total meaning of history revealed in Christ. This recovery of the mission of the church requires a concern for identification with the peoples who are involved in the revolutionary struggles to change existing power structures. This approach presupposes that the work of Christ and his kingdom is discernible in the secular, social, and political revolutions of our time and that the church's function is to discern it and to witness to it and to participate in God's work in changing the world.

Even though the institutional church has failed, its message and misssion have provided the ferment for the new struggle for humanity which has produced signs and anticipations of the kingdom in the revolutions of our time.[62] This does not mean that faith is reduced to an ideology of the revolution, but that faith should relate itself dynamically to ideologies of the revolution to make them more human and realistic, through bringing them under the criterion and power of the New Humanity in Christ.[63]

What Is God Doing?

A reaction to these bold statements was inevitable. H. H. Wolf was concerned about what he considered to be parallels with Christianity in Nazi Germany.[64] The church, Wolf holds, cannot see secular history as a source of revelation. The only source of revelation is the Word of God. Christians do not listen to the Word *in* a given situation; rather, they listen to the Word *for* a given situation.[65] The Word was given once for all, and God's complete revelation has been given with that Word—once for all.

Wolf fears that Thomas allows the social efforts and events which occur in a social revolution to decide what the gospel is, instead of leaving that decision to the gospel itself. Even if it is true that the gospel can help to make human life fuller and richer both ethically and materially ("but always in the sense of Matt. 6:33") Thomas's statements remind Wolf of the theology of the *Deutsche Christentum*. The Barmen Declaration was an apologia against this theology. It attacked the "Christ idea" of the German Christians—an idea which could be directly associated with ever-new manifestations in the events, persons, and institutions of history once it is separated from its source, the revelation of God as testified to in the Bible. World history, Wolf contends, is never a binding manifestation of Jesus Christ and can never be substituted for the unique revelation of the Christ of the Bible. The world as such will always be a rebellious world and though "provisional," "temporary" changes may be brought about, such changes "will never bring about the full kingdom of God, which in its perfection can only be understood as a gift of the Lord when He comes again."[66]

Wolf fears that the "promises of Christ" that become clear in these revolutions will acquire the character of revelation, as was the case with the concept of history of the German Christians," . . .and this ultimately also determines how the gospel and the presence of Christ are ready to be interpreted—if that is still necessary."[67]

The questions raised in the revolutionary situation are not always the right questions, even if they do reveal what the gospel *also* says, and Wolf is sure that in Thomas's thinking the questions which arise in the revolutionary situation in Asia and Africa in reality dictate what the Christian message for that situation is.[68]

Wolf returns once more to the question of the search for a

fuller and richer human life in revolutionary change which Thomas regards as commensurate with the gospel:

Does not the gospel or the presence of Christ guarantee a fuller and richer human life even when no change has yet taken place in the bad moral and social conditions of personal and social life? For . . . the gospel is ultimately the message and promise of man's reconciliation with God through forgiveness, which is guaranteed through the death and resurrection of Christ.[69]

Another critic of Thomas was A. G. Honig.[70] Honig agrees with Thomas on the point of the Lordship of Christ in the world, and he concedes that Christ is indeed also at work through historical events. Still, the way Thomas speaks of Christ's acts in history, Honig regards as "unbiblical." Honig argues that the Bible speaks of Christ's acts in history in terms of reconciliation, resurrection, of Christ being seated at the right hand of the Father ruling over all and living in the church through the Spirit. "In this way," he concludes, "Christ is doubtlessly present and active in the world of today."[71] Like Wolf, Honig finds that Thomas fosters "the heresy that there can be other sources of revelation besides the Word of God."[72] Honig finds it extremely difficult to believe that the changes in Asia and Africa are also the work of Christ.

Honig firmly believes that the gospel is the only norm by which historical events should be judged. These events are not divine revelation; they are rather an appeal to obedience. Thomas, according to Honig, does not discriminate sufficiently between the way God acts as Creator and Keeper of the world as Lord of all and his redemptive deeds in Jesus Christ. The first (God is Lord) is a confession of faith; the second is revealed to man.[73] Honig denies Thomas's assertion that Christians are able to discern through faith the promises of Christ within historical events so that they can react positively and critically to these events:

Somehow there is some knowledge of freedom; . . . somehow people may understand that the feudal societal structures are dehumanizing; . . . but nowhere do people *really* know about these things, for man is sinful and cannot (and will not) do else than suppress truth and justice.[74]

In this situation, according to Honig, God has called his church to proclaim the redeeming love of Christ which will gather all things into one, according to Scripture. The "Christian awareness" Thomas speaks of, Honig considers insufficient: The gospel is the only norm by which historical events must be tested if our expectations of the kingdom of God are not to end "in expecting the *fata morganas* which the devil conjures up before our eyes."[75] We must be well aware, Honig warns, of the powers of the anti-Christ in every situation and every revolution.

In his defense, Thomas begins by questioning the way Wolf applied the Barmen Declaration to the situations Thomas was discussing. Careful reading convinces us that Thomas is not really guilty of what he has been accused of. The Barmen Declaration was a heroic act of confession against institutionalized idolatry, and the whole church everywhere has received its impact. But its refutation was primarily in the field of religion and not of politics. Thomas holds that Christ is present and active *in* the world. But if Christ is *in* the situation, he is not *of* it but *for* it. The kingdom of God, understood as the final consummation of all things in Christ, or its partial realization here and now, cannot be confined only to the church. The question Christians should ask is, what are the creaturely (i.e., the human) purposes to which God has awakened the peoples of Asia and Africa through the modern revolutions; and what are the manifestations of the spiritual rebellion against God within them which betray these creaturely purposes.[76] Nowhere does Thomas give historical events the authority of divine revelation. He was merely pointing out that the confession "Christ the Lord" must have the consequence that Christ is also at work in history, even in those events where demonic powers are working against him.

Thomas does not deny the powers of the anti-Christ, but he holds on to the truth that Christ is the Risen Lord and therefore ultimately stronger than the forces that rebel against him.

Honig agrees with Thomas that Christ does not work through the church alone. Yet Honig makes the remarkable statement that it is a special temptation for Christians in Asia and Africa to see Christ at work in *their* situation whereas Dutch Christians *cannot but* see what is happening in Europe as connected with what Christ is doing through the gospel.[77]

What must one conclude from this statement? That Christ is working more, or more recognizably, in Europe than elsewhere? Also less than clear is Honig's explanation of the presence of Christ in the world. To explain this he uses a metaphysical manner of speech, obscuring the problem rather than clarifying it. Thomas has stated simply that the social upheavals, inasmuch as they serve the search for true humanity, work toward the fulfilment of the promises of Christ in the gospel. Where human liberation is effected, Christ is at work. Honig says: Christ is seated at the right hand of the Father; he rules over the world and lives in the church through his Spirit. This is true, but it does not answer the pressing question of how Christ is at work in the world of today and how Christians in revolutionary situations have to discern his presence. Nor does it answer the questions raised by the activity of Christians within the process of liberation.

Thomas never intended to make the gospel subject to "the situation" as Wolf claims. On the contrary, Thomas explicitly states that as the Word and deed (!) of God, the gospel transcends and judges all cultures and situations. There is therefore no point in Wolf's reminding Thomas that the Christian listens to the Word of God for every situation.

Thomas claimed that where liberation is effected (the "new humanity"), where true human authenticity is served, it is commensurate with the gospel. In their discussions neither Wolf nor Honig denied this important point. What they did, however, was to endeavor to contrast God's actions as Creator and Sustainer and his actions as Redeemer and Reconciler through Jesus Christ. This separation we hold contrary to biblical thinking. It originates in the western dualism we have previously discussed, and it clearly shows that this dualism leads to the excessive spiritualization Gutiérrez warned against, which results in breaking up the wholeness of life and in dichotomizing God's deed of liberation (separating liberation from salvation).

In contrast, the theology of liberation contends that Yahweh, Creator and Sustainer of the world, is the same God who, in bringing Israel out of slavery, created for himself a new people. His acts in history are repeatedly described as acts of re-creation, a re-creation which finds its consummation in Jesus the Messiah. Black Theology denies the kind of separation that one is forced to make if one accepts this dualistic pattern of thought:

According to Matt. 10:29ff, God is at work in everything that happens; He is the Lord of History, who is creating and sustaining the world all the time. That is a statement of the Christian faith although there is no evidence for it. At the same time, however, God is at work in the unique historical event of his Son—an event which is assumed in its effects into the Lordship of the risen Christ who continues to be active through the means He has ordered, forgiving sins, liberating men from death, bringing reconciliation and beginning the new mankind in Him. These two different aspects of God's action must be borne in mind.[78]

This dichotomy, so evident in the quotation from Wolf, effectively widens the gap between our experience of faith and our experience in history, creating a totally unnecessary tension which can only be dissolved in pietistic formulations. Therefore, Thomas is correct in saying that Wolf, while defending Barmen, is actually unwilling to go forward along the path of Christian discernment in history indicated by Barmen. "He [Wolf] had gone into the narrow pietism and preoccupation with religion to the exclusion of the secular which he himself condemns."[79] Wolf finds it necessary to remind Thomas that the kingdom of God can never be brought about by the changes of revolution, etc. Thomas, however, has never ventured such a statement. He has never, either explicitly or implicitly, identified the kingdom of God with the ideologies and revolutions in Asia and Africa, in anything he said in New Delhi (or elsewhere). Point 3 of his "discoveries" ends thus:

So the mission of the Church is not to save itself from the revolutions of our time, but to discern the promise and judgment of Christ in them and to witness to His kingdom in them, *waiting for the day of its final consummation.*[80]

What is the nature of this Christian discernment? Thomas answers as follows: A Christian's responsible participation in the political realm requires discrimination between the creaturely and the idolatrous, leading to an affirmation of the creaturely (the human) and resistance to the idolatrous (the source of the inhuman) in the power of the Holy Spirit.[81] This Honig denies. In the New Testament, he holds, the apostles did not see Christ act in secular history, neither in the functioning of law in the Roman Empire, nor in the welfare or the science of the society in which they were living then:

No redeeming and reconciling work of Christ is pointed out in all this so that the faith of the Church could discern (the acts of Christ) and thus stand positively and critically in state and society.[82]

We contend that Thomas is right. The apostles, deeply absorbed in their expectation that the Lord would soon come, had concentrated more on preparing the church for this event than for participation in the realm of politics.

But this was not Honig's last word. In a later publication, he grapples extensively with this problem and there he comes to the following conclusion. We quote him at length:

In the new Man Jesus Christ the new humanity is given. . . . That is why He commands us to participate in the struggle for justice. Pity and charity are not enough. Whereas all things are reconciled with God in Christ, the peace and righteousness of his kingdom must become undeniably clear. *We are called to discern where Christ is at work for that purpose. In political developments, in revolutions and social upheavals, in the development of technology and science, in ideologies and living faiths, in the struggle against racism and war, in the struggle for democratic freedom, through the work of international organizations, in violent actions and in nonviolent movements, Christ is there and He works toward the final consummation.*[83]

Honig goes on to say that one can be sure that rebellion against Christ is also working through historical events and this complicates hearing the voice of Christ among the many others. Every situation is profoundly ambiguous and interpretation is a very risky business. But the Christian, Honig says, has no choice. He cannot be neutral or claim that he is "not involved," for Christ is in these developments.[84] Interpretation can never be separated from commitment, from being "engaged in," and therefore effectively silences all theoretical discussion on the progress of history and peoples:

We are involved in history with Christ and are called to find our way with Him amidst historical events. This means continually making an interpretative choice: for Him and against all rebellion against Christ, even if this choice means rebellion against the established order.[85]

We have no difficulty at all in giving our full support to this view posed by Honig. Indeed, he succinctly formulates here the risk of faith which Christians have to take in order to be genuine.

Once More: What Is God Doing?

Although this very difficult question of the acts of God in history and the will of God is a question that can be asked only within the community of believers, it concerns not only that community. The church is the church in the world and whatever God is doing in the church he is also doing in the world. Paul Lehmann pointed out that the question, "Does God work in history?" is inescapably linked with the question, "What am I to do in the world?" The answer is: the will of God.[86]

Yet, the will of God is not simply "written in the law" or in tradition. This is not a simple matter, but this much is clear to us: What God requires people to do is totally inexplicable apart from the dynamics of the divine activity of God of which the inseparable context is the liberation of his people in the Exodus-event.[87]

To ask simply: "What am I to do?" and simply to reply: "the

will of God," says Lehmann, ignores both what God is doing in the world and the ethical reality of the human situation. The fact is that outside of the context of the divine activity it makes no sense to talk about the will of God; and within the context of the divine activity the question about the will of God exposes the paradoxical character of our ethical situation.[88] Nonetheless, we are inescapably involved in what God is doing in the world. The activity of God cannot be confined to the church, to believers alone. Both believer and unbeliever, says Lehmann, are in the same ethical situation because both are confronted by Christ's liberating activity and his ethical demands. But for believers the Lordship of Christ is revealed; in the world (i.e., among unbelievers) it is hidden. But

the difference between believers and unbelievers is not defined by church membership, or even, in the last analysis, by baptism. The difference is defined by imaginative and behavioral sensitivity to what God is doing in the world to make and to keep human life human, to achieve . . . the new humanity.[89]

In any case, this liberating activity of God is the context within which the question about his acts in history and his will is to be asked and understood. The reality of God's acts in the world can be understood only on the grounds of his revelation, on the grounds of the testimony about him in the Old and New Testaments. His liberating deeds are manifested not only within the bosom of the church but in universal history. Christians suffering under colonialism and oppression have experienced that the churches of the rich nations and their theological and ecclesiastical reproductions in the "Third World" were not able, theologically and otherwise, to challenge, much less to overcome the ideologies of oppression and dependency which had become intertwined with their understanding and proclamation of the gospel.[90] It was this realization which more than anything else had opened the eyes of Christians in the "Third World" to the fact that the activity of God cannot be confined to the church.

This divine action is not static, but dynamic. It does not

annul human history and responsibility but rather enhances it, giving it a new dimension and a new meaning.

BY BREAD ALONE?
BLACK THEOLOGY AND BLACK POWER

Reconciliation and Power

Having come so far, we must consider briefly power in its relation to the themes of reconciliation, love, and suffering. Some have argued that the Christian does not seek power, that the power of Christ lay essentially in his powerlessness on the Cross. Is the stress on socio-political liberation therefore not a decidedly one-sided desire to live "by bread alone"?

A. J. Rasker speaks of the "power of the Son of Man" which is the "secret of the salvation of humanity and of the truth."[91] What does he mean? Truth, Rasker says, is knowing in the midst of fear and menace of the "gentle powers" which shall win in the end: reconciliation, forgiveness, sacrifice. He then goes on to speak of the "powerless Christ" who, in his power-lessness, nonetheless possesses the only authority—an inward authority given him by the power of love. It is this love which is stronger than death. According to Rasker, Christians should strive towards this powerless power.[92]

Black Theology does not for one moment deny the validity of this argumentation, but we must emphasize again the framework within which the gospel message comes to people, namely, that of liberation toward the wholeness of life. The ultimate question really is: What is the responsibility *toward liberation* the gospel places upon us? Reconciliation, forgiveness and sacrifice find their meaning only when regarded against the background of God's liberating and reconciling acts in Jesus Christ.

Liberation and reconciliation presuppose one another. It is the Liberator-Messiah who heals, forgives, restores, and reconciles. In the Bible the central character of reconciliation corresponds with the wholeness of God's liberation.[93] In order to be reconciled with others, black people first have to be reconciled with themselves. This means consciously overcoming the self-alienation that has grown out of the rejection of black humanity, creating what Manas Buthelezi has called "dominion over the created black self." This calls for a new relation with whites built on solidarity and what Jesse Jackson has aptly called "redistributing the pain." In socio-political terms, reconciliation is possible only after the establishment of righteousness and social justice, after power, rights, and responsibilities are no longer the privilege of a happy few, but shared by all.

H. Wiersinga opens a perspective which is meaningful for black/white relationships. Reconciliation, according to him, exposes not only evil itself, but also the covering-up of evil. For example, the horrendous reality of racism in South Africa is hidden behind the innocence of the *Apartheid* ideal, the "goodwill" or "good intention" of the oppressor, or the pretension of a civil religion.

"The root of the evil," Wiersinga contends, "does not lie with the principle of guilt as such, but with the guilt that is veiled."[94] Indeed, for as Rollo May had correctly pointed out, it is exactly this innocence which serves as a shield behind which people foster a sense of childishness.[95] Thus they remain "unaware" of the evil they themselves have created and help to maintain. Refusing to take responsibility upon themselves, they hide behind those "in authority," or behind the "structures" or the "ideology," leaving, for example, "politics to the politicians." Precisely because such people refuse to share the responsibility of guilt, they are unable to share the responsibility for change toward reconciliation.

Suffering and Power

The New Testament exhortations have been much misused with regard to the oppressed. One of the central biblical texts in this regard has always been 1 Peter 2:18, which reads:

Slaves must be respectful and obedient to their masters, not only when they are kind and gentle, but also when they are unfair.

Some introductory remarks: The wider context of this letter

of Peter is the all-encompassing work of Christ. In those days, slavery was considered a "normal" social phenomenon, which the Christian church did not ignore. The stand of the New Testament church on this issue *as a matter of principle* was clear. Because of the freedom in Christ, the barriers between masters and slaves no longer exist. Social differences are transcended by the fellowship in Christ (Philemon; 1 Cor. 7:21–23; Gal. 3:28). Within the Christian community, slaves were accepted on equal footing with their masters. Whatever a person's social status, they were all baptized by the Holy Spirit into one body (1 Cor. 12:13; Col. 3:11). We may conclude, then, that the principle of slavery was unacceptable to the New Testament church, although it must be said that the structural reality of slavery seemed to have escaped their attention.

In the light of these considerations, M. H. Bolkenstein, discussing Peter's exhortation, observes: "This is clearly meant for the slaves and not for the master." And he adds, "Does this mean that 'masters' did not exist within the church?"[96] According to Bolkenstein, Peter's warning had a clear motivation: Slaves who refused to accept their social position would cause disruption and so discredit the gospel and the church. It was therefore better to suffer than try to end slavery in an arbitrary fashion.[97] New Testament scholars agree that Peter did not propagate slavery.[98] He was addressing a particular church in a particular situation. His position was both understandable and necessary and can certainly not be generalized.[99] The apostle's call upon Christ is intended to draw attention to Christ's suffering, which in itself was a liberating act toward reconciliation, which always implies authentic transformation. Peter had more in mind than an "incidental," formal abolition of slavery. He was, rather, "concerned with a total, radical renewal of human relations and mankind."[100]

But we must say more about the apostle's parallel with the suffering of Christ. This is definitely not a glorification of suffering; neither is this an expression of some kind of Christian masochism. All suffering is evil and as such not in accord with God's purposes for people. Manas Buthelezi makes the valuable distinction between "oppressive suffering" and "redemptive" suffering. Suffering enforced upon people by others, by willful inflicting of pain, crippling to one's resolve and initiative, is oppressive suffering. It is the result of violence; it is evil and should be removed.[101]

Counsel to endure this kind of suffering is creating a cult, so that suffering becomes an end in itself, a god unto itself. To liken this kind of suffering to the suffering of Christ, says Buthelezi, "is a gross manifestation of a callous conscience."

Redemptive suffering, on the other hand, is suffering after the model of Christ to save others. This suffering is not an end in itself but is endured in the course of a struggle to realize the well being of others. The power to endure this suffering comes out of love and seeks to realize the objective that lies beyond suffering, namely, liberation. This is the suffering the followers of Christ must bear, but bear manifestly, thereby ultimately serving the liberation of self and the other:

If physical death is the price that a man must pay to free his children and his white brethren from a permanent death of the spirit, then nothing could be more redemptive.[102]

Love and Power

We now come to a theme we have already touched upon in our discussion of power. We have noticed that God's love is an active deed of liberation manifested in divine power. We have also noticed that it is not necessary to contrast love and power. Martin King's dictum is both valuable and true: "Love without power is sentimental and anemic; power without love is reckless and abusive." Power without love is essentially unauthentic; it becomes cruel and ultimately demonic.

Love and power come together in the one loving activity of God. Through God's love for black people, James Cone writes, they are given the power to *become*.[103] Love and power are interrelated, and Paul Tillich holds, correctly, that "love is the foundation, not the negation, of power."[104] In any case, the understanding of power we have expounded thus far presupposes love as a central element in the exercise of power. Let us turn for a moment to the power of Jesus. Jesus' views on power are very clearly put in his reply to the request of the mother of the sons of Zebedee that her two sons be seated next to Jesus in his kingdom (Matt. 20:20–28): "You know that among the pagans the rulers lord it over them, and their great men make their authority felt. This is not to happen among you. No, anyone who wants to be great among you must be your servant, and anyone who wants to be first among you must be your slave—just as the Son of Man came not to be served but to serve, and to give his life as a ransom for many."

In Jesus of Nazareth the power of God is revealed, as well as the power of those who, through their faith in this divine power, are no longer impressed by the powers and principalities of this world. They know for certain: God is Lord. Their enslavement by earthly powers has ended in their liberation by the Messiah. The life of Jesus was a manifestation of power and freedom which allowed him to speak and live in a way that was completely new. He has no need of violence and aggression, nor of manipulation, for his words revealed an indisputable authority: He does not have to prove himself. This authority causes turmoil and fear among those who do not accept him; those who do experience wholeness and liberation.

They receive their sight; they are freed from guilt, fear and greed: They are saved! When Jesus acts, he does not demonstrate a worldly power, as he openly admits to Pilate (John 18:36). But at the same time his is a power that cannot be denied by the world, for through this power the world can be changed. This is the power that Jesus invites those who believe in him to share, this authentic power that by its very nature does not force, intimidate, or threaten. It is a creative, humanizing service toward liberation.

This view on power is diametrically opposed to that of the existing order. The Messiah is Lord to people. His power liberates people; it does not subjugate and humiliate them. It gives life; it does not destroy. His is the power of love, justice, and liberation. This is the power that has been given to him in all its fullness (Matt. 28:19) so that *this* power be the final authority by which all power in human hands shall be measured. He who is first was willing to become our slave, to give himself so that we may have life and share in his life, his love, service, and glory.

Conclusion

We bring this discussion to its conclusion. Power, we have said, is the courage to be, to have dominion over the created self. This courage is grounded in Christ in whom black people are given the new humanity and from whom they receive the power to be. Knowing who they are, blacks have the freedom to become what they should be. Thus, Black Power is indeed not the antithesis of the gospel. On this point, Cone has our agreement.

There is, however, a danger of complete identification with Black Power's political program (in all its expressions!) in which we cannot sympathetically follow theologians like Cleage, Washington, and Maimela. James Cone is moving away from this absolute position he held previously when he writes:

Unless we black theologians can make an adequate distinction between divine revelation and human aspirations, there is nothing to keep Black Theology from identifying God's will with anything black people should decide to do at any given historical moment.[105]

This danger Cone mentions is evident in the thinking of Maimela and Cleage, who identify God's will with everything blacks do in effecting their liberation as well as with black culture.[106] In contrast to this way of thinking, we reiterate the thesis that although Christ enters a culture to fulfil all that is good in it, he also enters to judge all that is dehumanizing and demeaning in it.

The gospel of Jesus Christ, to repeat the words of M. M. Thomas, should not be identified with any one culture, political order, social ideology, or moral system. As the word and deed of God transcending all cultures, it is the divine power for their judgment and redemption. Black Power is commensurate with the gospel to the extent that it serves the liberation and the authentic humanity of black people. Inasmuch as Black Power serves the new humanity through liberation and the wholeness of life out of which flow justice, peace, reconciliation, and community, Black Power is God's work and an authentic Christian witness to God's presence in the world today.

G. T. Rothuizen defines ehtics as "creating some order in life."[107] He emphasizes that this "order" does not refer to the "order of the *status quo*," but to the creation of an order in which the fulfilment of human life is realized:

The Christian knows that the real issue [in Christian ethics] is the kingdom of God . . . and he tries with all his might to bring heaven on earth—or to bring it back on earth, for has it not been there once already, in Bethlehem, among the animals and the poor . . . ? He definitely does not want a pie-in-the-sky gospel, but a social gospel. At the same time, however, he recognizes that this could never be fully realized in this life.[108]

Black Theology realizes that Black Power does not have the "last word," nor can it offer "final solutions." In other words, the forces of Black Power will never bring about the fullness of the kingdom of God. This fact, however, will not deter blacks in their efforts to transform the world through their prophetic witness and total commitment to the liberation of the oppressed.

In the next chapter ideology and the relationship between ideology and theology will be scrutinized more closely, in the course of which we shall have to determine to what extent Black Theology (or our understanding of it, cf. chapter 1) is susceptible to ideology.

CHAPTER FOUR

Haven't We Heard All This Before?

On Ideology

If the Word of God is not the fire that renews us, other fires shall devour us; if the Word of God is not the hammer that crushes rocks, other hammers shall destroy us. Listen, O people of God!
                                                    Beyers Naudé, 1963

Every Church, all Christians, face the question whether they serve Christ and his serving work alone, or at the same time also the powers of inhumanity. "No man can serve two masters, God and Mammon."
                                    Mission Conference, Bangkok, 1973

IDEOLOGY

The discussion in the previous chapter brought us close to our subject in this chapter. We've heard in Wolf's objections to the statements of M.M. Thomas and in his own reference to the German Christians the allusion to recent history. Wolf seems to ask: Haven't we heard all this before? The same question can be (and has been) put to Black Theology. Is Black Theology not really (or is it more than) an ideology of blackness? Or put another way, does not Black Theology repeat the mistakes of white theology by operating within an ideological framework?

There are different ways of speaking about ideology. Ideology can be seen as a system of ideas, a blueprint, a plan to reach certain goals in the socio-political field, for instance a

99

"five-year" or "ten-year plan," frequently designed by developing nations for socio-economic development. Here the term ideology is used in a positive sense.

In quite another sense, ideology has a negative connotation. The word was first popularized during the French Enlightenment.[1] For the ideologists (those who used the word positively) like Antoine Destutt, "ideology" as the "formation of ideas" is rooted in people's rational nature and provides a sound basis for their actions in history.[2] During the same period, however, the word "ideology" assumed a pejorative meaning. It came to denote "idle, subversive speculations, completely divorced from reality."[3]

This negative connotation was extended by Karl Marx[4] and from him has acquired still another meaning. Ideology now denotes the fact that "there could be no pure theory." Behind every social theory, class interests are involved. Therefore, all political theories reflect the social situations and the class interests of the oppressing classes. In Marx's thinking, ideology became the pathology of human knowledge which strays away from the real processes of life, endeavors to cover up the extent of human maladjustment and alienation. For example, in reality the workers no longer regard social forces as a power in which they share, but as a foreign force which enslaves them. Ideology conceals the economic and material origin of this enslavement and alienation. Even more so, it justifies enslavement at three levels, according to Marx's later writings: the level of economics, the level of the state, and the level of religion.[5]

The results of the sociology of knowledge brought to light, however, that it is not possible for any person, even one of the oppressed classes, to theorize without having been influenced by his particular situation. Moreover, the evolution of the function of ideology has shown that Marxism could nowhere find the guarantee that its own ideology will not also reflect the interests, if not of a class, then of a country which is unique.

Karl Mannheim draws a distinction between ideology and utopia.[6] He defines ideology as the conservative justification of the status quo and utopia as a creative outlook which transcends the social reality *and wants to change it.* Mannheim insists that the difference between ideology and utopia becomes manifest precisely in this element: Ideologies may transcend reality but they always justify the status quo; on the other hand,

only those orientations transcending reality will be referred to by us as utopian which, when they pass over into conduct, tend to shatter, either partially or wholly, the order of things prevailing at the time.[7]

As a system, ideology benefits power in that it is an idealization either of the present or of the future—an idealization which consolidates the existing power structure. It is clear that Mannheim did not intend to return to "ideology" its positive meaning.

There are others who want to do that. Risto Lehtonen criticizes what he calls "a strong undercurrent among Christians of various traditions" which tend to contrast Christian faith to ideology.[8]

These Christians judge ideologies negatively, as substitutes for religion. To be sure, Lehtonen says, there are ideologies which can never be reconciled with the Christian faith. Racism, for instance, is such an ideology. But today, the "mere negation of the relationship and identification with ideology is obviously an inadequate response for Christians."[9] An ideology which presents its claims in a totalitarian fashion is a distortion of the gospel. As with racism, this is also the case with much of the "Christian ideology,"

which is still alive where Churches and Christians rise to defend their privileges and even their political control over men and societies.[10]

Identification with such an ideology is not permissible. Lehtonen, however, recognizes a twofold danger in the identification of the Christian faith with any ideology: that of sanctifying or even absolutizing the ideology and that of distorting the gospel by subjecting it to a closed system. In other words, the gospel must be identified with an ideology, but with an ideology which aims at human and social transformation and human liberation, and definitely not with those ideologies that have caused past horrors and are still responsible for

continued destruction, oppression and mass disasters perpetuated by the more subtle ideologies of the affluent world, often under the pretext of preserving freedom, law and order. The presence and the potential of this new ruthlessness need to be uncovered and its ideological mask revealed.[11]

Albert Stüttgen formulated five criteria by which to recognize an ideology:

1. It claims absoluteness and exclusiveness—a holistic preten-sion, Stütten calls it, to know all of reality, an unwillingness to be corrected, and a certainty that it could never be wrong.
2. There is a complete schism with the real world, the world in which people have their daily experiences. The experiences of others do not affect the ideology; neither do the results of scientific research.
3. The third is complementary to the second: The ideology does not allow for the possibility of new experience. It lives within a closed, isolated, fossilized system of ideas and has a mortal fear of change.
4. The ideology lives on presuppositions, but these are pur-posely kept unclear and vague. They are neither illumi-nated nor subjected to honest criticism.
5. The ideology needs prejudices and clichés to survive.[12]

At this point Stüttgen notes that prejudices as such are not forbidden, but they must be constantly tested and subjected to honest and open criticism. When Stüttgen speaks of ideology as a theory or a doctrine bent on maintaining itself instead of serving the truth, we agree.[13]

We understand ideology as an idea or system of ideas, a doctrine or theory or system of doctrines or theories used to justify and perpetuate existing structures of injustice. We note furthermore that ideology does not only constitute theory but also praxis, that the self-justifying character of an ideology is usually hidden from the group using the ideology, and that there is a relation between the ideology and the socio-political reality in which power is legitimized.[14]

Of great theological import is what J. Verkuyl and André Dumas have already pointed out, namely, the strange resemblance of ideologies to religious faith.[15] Dumas writes:

This very similarity means that the ideologies are formidable competitors with faith. . . . The ideologies try to replace the very content of faith, either in the extreme form of total ideologies like Marxism, or in the diluted form of an ideological ethos.[16]

If one recognizes this, it remains very problematic indeed to speak of the identification of Christian faith with an ideology either as a matter of course or as a necessity (see Lehtonen). This similarity makes religion extremely vulnerable to an ideological takeover, something which has happened often enough in history. The question that arises, therefore, is: When does Christian theology become an ideology?

THEOLOGY AND IDEOLOGY

The tension between theology and ideology is an old one and was already manifested in the struggle of the true prophets in Israel against the ideological onslaught on the faith of Israel by the rich and privileged and the false prophets. Of particular significance in this regard is what C. J. Labuschagne writes in a study on ideology and prophetic witness in Israel.[17] The national ideology of the people *(volksideologie)*, Labuschagne writes, is an ideology conceived by the nation of Israel, peculiar to that nation and completely in the service of that nation. Its first characteristic is its ethnocentric, national-political religiosity. The religious leaders of the people are not bound to obedience to Yahweh, but have become no more than "executives of the will of the nation" and their primary task is to give theological sanction to the establishment:

Not Yahweh and his will, but the nation and the will of the nation, based on majority opinion and the "demands of the times," stood in the center.[18]

One can also substitute "the nation" with any privileged group in society that uses the gospel to defend its own interests and its own position in society. Such a theology has severed its relation with biblical revelation and stands primarily in relation to the particular group or nation it serves. It loses sight of the central message of the Bible and becomes intent on the preservation, perpetuation, and justification of existing oppressive structures, because they serve the interests of the particular group.

We shall try to elucidate this in the light of three examples. The first is from the nineteenth century. It is an extract from a report by a certain Reverend M.C. Vos who worked in South Africa at the beginning of the nineteenth century. He relates his method of persuading the white settlers to allow him to preach the gospel to their slaves:

It is only natural that your slaves, through religious education, should become better people, not the other way around. Let me try to explain. Among your slaves, so I have observed, there are different nationalities. Please try to put yourself in their place and try to see things from their point of view:

I am a poor slave, but I was born free. Peddlers of human flesh have stolen me from my free country, from my dear parents, my dear wife, my children, my brothers and sisters. I have no hope of ever seeing them alive again. Tyrants have brought me to this country and even on the journey to this house of bondage I would have preferred to die, were it not that chains rendered me helpless. Here I was sold like a piece of cattle and now I am a slave, forced to do all that my master bids me, knowing that the slightest sign of disobedience will bring severe punishment.

Just imagine this to be your position. What would you do? Would you not refuse to work? Wouldn't you be restless, sad, rebellious, and disobedient? The settler was moved. "I have never thought of it in this way," he confessed. "Who knows to what desperate deeds I would have been driven if I were a slave!" Well [Rev. Vos went on] if you leave your slaves like this, uneducated and ignorant, it won't be long before they will think this way, and who knows what terrible extremes they might resort to! But if we could have the opportunity to teach them that there is such a thing as divine providence, that nothing happens without the will of God, that this God is a God of order and that just as they have to serve their earthly masters, so their masters must serve God. Just as they are punished by their masters when disobedient, so their masters are punished by God if they disobey him. If we also make clear to them that the things which seem unbearable to us are the will of God for our good; and that indeed, if they had stayed in their free country they would never have heard about the saving grace of our Lord and on dying would have been lost for ever. Now fortunately they were brought to a Christian country where they have the opportunity to learn to know our Lord and Savior Jesus Christ, who is able to give them eternal happiness. Once they understand this, they will change. Instead of entertaining rebellious thoughts, they will say: If this is the case, I will be content with what I am and I will do my best to serve my master obediently and with joy.

"Why," exclaimed the man, "have we not been told these things before? I must confess my ignorance and from now on will advise one and all to allow their slaves religious education."[19]

We move on to our second example. J. Sperna Weiland—who defines ideology as "a pattern of thoughts through which a group of people or an individual define the meaning of reality and in doing this define themselves and justify their own position, their own actions and their own interest in the world"[20]—contends that we should read history and theology with the question in mind whether there is a "text behind the text." We believe that Sperna Weiland is right.

Theology is never objective or "neutral." It always presupposes and is influenced by certain interests. This is what lies behind the text.[21] If, as Black Theology holds, the truth of biblical revelation is God's liberation of the oppressed, then theology inspired by an oppression-mindedness is not biblical theology but an ideology. Any theology which does not take God's liberation of the poor and the oppressed as its central point of departure thereby excludes itself effectively from being a witness to the divine presence in the world. The point is, therefore, not whether theology is determined by interests, but whether it is being determined by the interests of the poor and the oppressed or by those of the oppressor. With this in mind, Cone quite explicitly calls white theology an ideology, and rightly so.[22]

Working with his definition of ideology and his "text behind the text" theory, Sperna Weiland contributes to our discussion by investigating the theology of Rudolf Bultmann. This is of utmost importance, for the theology of Bultmann presents itself as a "critical" theology, questioning traditional theological conceptions and thinking, introducing terms like *ent-mythologiserung,* i.e., the process of purging Christian theology of the myths and legends which had grown around the original, simple truth. The question Sperna Weiland puts is this: Is the theology of Bultmann, however critical vis-à-vis traditional theological thinking, not essentially an uncritical ideology?[23]

Bultmann, according to Sperna Weiland, believes that "sin" is no more than living in terms of survival, of self-preservation. To be really free is to be free from sin, free from the "world" and the concerns of the world. Where people are free, the hold of earthly concerns is broken. In its place comes a new openness for the *Unweltliche,* the other-worldly reality of which we cannot say much but out of which we may live. Using Bonhoeffer's distinction between "faith" and "religion," Sperna Weiland concludes that Bultmann's existential theology is "religious theology" which places us in a situation where we are overwhelmed by a metaphysical longing for peace which we cannot find in the "world." This peace comes rather from the *Unweltliche* to make the believer free.

The essence of Bultmann's theology and the danger it entails was pointed out some time ago by Johann Metz.[24] Metz warned against this "new theology" which tried to counteract the Enlightenment by what he called "privatization" of faith and theology. Metz explicitly named the theology of Bultmann which, in his mind, makes use of "intimate," "a-political" terminology, doomed to circle within the narrowness of the I-Thou relationship, denying the existence of the socio-political reality, a relationship wherein the proclamation of the gospel can only be translated into a personal appeal.[25]

Rubem Alves comes to the same conclusions in his examination of Bultmann's theological program.[26] In Bultmann's theology, Alves discovered, the objective world remains a threat. Human liberation is a subjective experience, a liberation from the world and its concerns. This liberation bears the character of a new, inner self-understanding. The immediate consequence is that the objective is dismissed as totally devoid of significance and import for the task of making human life human in the world. This means, Alves writes, that we become de-historicized. Liberation consists of "being lifted out of" the realities of this life. Alves talks about a "kind of despair about the created world" so that hope is reduced "to a dimension of subjectivity without any import for the transformation of the world. Its hope (such as there is) does not create but abrogates history."[27]

Because salvation is, so to speak, locked up within the existence, the personal being of the believer, the socio-political reality does not lie within the horizon of this theology. Sperna Weiland comes to the conclusion that the theology of Bultmann is an ideology for the following reasons:

1. It serves the interest of a church which wishes to maintain itself by any means necessary in a world it no longer rules;
2. it serves the interests of groups that wield power in the world. It reacts positively to the existing system—any given system—on the presumption: give unto Caesar . . . ;
3. it serves the interests of a few believers, the interests of the middle-class, status quo church.

When the world of labor and politics is consigned to irrelevance by this overwhelming message of personal existential salvation, Sperna Weiland concludes, when it has become the "unreal world"; why should one try to change the world at all?[28] In this way, even a so-called critical theology can be used as a justification of the status quo.

We have mentioned a publication from 1947 in which a theological justification for the *Apartheid* ideology is ventured. Even today, Dutch Reformed theology still functions as a theological justification for *Apartheid*, and brings us to our third example. The so-called *Landman Report*, an extensive report on race relations in South Africa commissioned by the General Synod of the white Dutch Reformed church, offers a few remarkable instances.[29] The Report accepts *Apartheid* as sanctioned by the Word of God. Nowhere, however, is there a sign that black people who suffer under this system have had the right to voice their opinion before the commission. Nowhere does one find a thorough critique of the validity of the white government's policy and its implications. The Report nowhere questions the fact that this policy is forced by less than four million whites on almost twenty million black people who were denied the right to share in the decision. Nowhere in the Report is there recognition of the fact that the people who suffer under *Apartheid* (and even some whites!) regard this system as unchristian and evil.

The Report's treatment of Christian ethics is invalid, because it forces the Christian ethic into the framework of *Apartheid* and subjects it to the national ideology, instead of subjecting the ideology to the critique of God's liberating Word.[30] In this way, for example, the Report admits that there is no evidence that Scripture prohibits racially mixed marriages. Yet it finds that "within the South African situation" the state has the right to forbid such marriages by law.[31]

This is in spite of the fact that the Synod accepts that the two people concerned love each other, that marriage is a particularly personal affair between two people and despite the fact that the Dutch Reformed formulary declares that "God brings the woman to the man with his own hand." It is clear to us that in this case, just as regards the question of "racially mixed church services and worship," it is not the Word of God, but the pseudoreligious ideology of *Apartheid* which has really become the norm for the white Dutch Reformed church.

There is an obvious anxious tone in the Report when it comes to the matter of racially mixed services. The Report expresses its "fear" that the "peace" in the church *and* in the nation would be disturbed by church services of such a nature.[32] Nowhere does the Report reflect the free and easy way in which the New Testament speaks about these matters. Rather we find that the principle of the unity of the church is undermined by its constant politically motivated misgivings. This is a pity. For it should be the church which should be sensitive and highly critical and questioning with regard to the cause of fear that such a natural Christian happening should be regarded a disturbance of the peace—both within the church and the nation.

Seen in its socio-political context, Juan Antonio Medina's injunction with regard to Puerto Rican society highlights the classic situation:

Ideology in the Puerto Rican class society serves to assure the exploiters' power over the exploited in two ways: On the one hand, it provides the framework necessary to enable the "super-exploited" victim of colonization to accept his own condition as a fact of life, as necessary for the common good, or as the will of God. On the other hand, ideology is useful to the bourgeois exploiters, as it helps them to accept and justify to their own satisfaction their position of control as desirable, pre-ordained, assigned as a moral duty, and even conferred upon them by God as a quasi-messianic mission.[33]

This is tragically true of the South African situation and the theology of the white Dutch Reformed church. A case in point is the damnable system of migrant labor which has become so essential to the economy of white South Africa. Dr. Francis Wilson has made a terrifying list of all the horrors caused by this system.[34] There is, he says, abundant evidence that the system of migrant labor as it exists in South Africa today can, and does, compel a young bride living with her husband who is working in some factory to leave him and go to some remote rural area that she has never seen and where she must live amongst her husband's people waiting to see him *once a year*, when he takes a brief holiday. Wilson continues:

This system can, and does, compel old people living amongst their friends and relatives in familiar surroundings where they have spent their entire working lives to endure resettlement in some distant place where they feel they have been cast off to die. This system can, and does, force a man who wants to build a home with his wife and children to live instead for all his working life in "bachelor" barracks, so far away from his loved ones that he sees them only briefly once a year, and his children grow up without his influence, regarding him as a stranger. One may close one's mind to these facts; one may dismiss them as being isolated casualties for the sake of a greater goal; but the harsh reality is that there are hundreds of thousands of people in South Africa who are cruelly affected in these ways.[35]

Had the white Dutch Reformed church not been so intent on justifying this evil system of *Apartheid*, it might have seen these bitter realities in which black people have to live. Had it not been so subordinate to the national ideology of white South Africa, it would have seen the plight of the weak and needy; it would have seen how the poor are being sold for a pair of sandals (Amos 2:6). Instead, the Report states, proving Juan Antonio Medina's point:

At present, the economic structure of the Republic of South Africa is so closely interwoven with the system of migrant labor that an abrupt termination is liable to cause disruption, not only within the economic system as a whole, but also within the economy of the homelands, which would result in privation for the migrant laborers and their families.[36]

By sanctioning the policy of *Apartheid*, the white Dutch Reformed church sanctions the atrocities of this system under which so many millions suffer. To be sure, the Report does suspect that people are suffering, but it regards these sufferings as no more than the result of "practical measures which for the sake of order are necessary in particular situations."[37]

The church, instead of proclaiming God's liberation for the poor and weak and his judgment on the oppressor, finds itself amongst those "who loathe justice and pervert what is right" (Mic. 3:9). In modern terms: it finds itself amongst those who distort cleverly, who "organize" because they have the power to, to the disadvantage of those who are in need. To "pervert what is right" means to disguise and veil reality, to harmonize contradictions and to arrange the facts to suit the theory and reality to suit the dogma.[38] The very fact that the white Dutch Reformed church so expressly wishes to be a *white church* makes of it a church of the rich and the powerful, justifying what is wrong, "abetting evil men so that no one renounces his evil-doing" (Jer. 23:14).

By Their Fruits Ye Shall Know Them

The unconditional identification of the South African white Reformed theology with the pseudoreligious ideology of *Apartheid* does not only result in theological excesses as illustrated above, but it also becomes evident in the spirit which pervades the church as such and which becomes manifest in utterances such as these:

The injunction to love thy neighbour . . . results in subversion of the modern order and leads to permissiveness in life. "Love thy neighbour" is idolatry and not in the Christian doctrine. We must love God above all things which means loving his image—ourselves and our neighbours, but He made us all different.[39]

While this is not official church doctrine, we contend that it is not at all surprsing that Afrikaners entertain such thoughts. The former editor of *Pro Veritate*, Roelf Meyer, put his finger on the spot when he commented: "Even God's commandments must be interpreted to serve the Afrikaner. The result is that God is in the Afrikaner's service, which in my view is blasphemy."[40] Again the similarity with the pseudoreligious national ideology of Israel as described by Labuschagne strikes us. Labuschagne observes:

The deity has been reduced to no more than a symbol—a vital symbol, but nonetheless merely a symbol—not only of the nation's glorious past (the liberation out of Egypt), but also of its future aspirations (in this case the possession of the promised land). Through all this, Yahweh did no more than play a role designated him by the grace of the nation within a situation where *the nation* had the final word.[41]

The conclusion of Roelf Meyer leads us to yet another question. Is this not also the case with Black Theology? This discussion is especially important within the South African context, where Black Theology faces a situation where the civil religion has become almost inseparable from the ideology of the Establishment. Our investigation of Black Theology and of ideology leads us to answer that question with an unqualified "no." Still, it is necessary to examine more closely the *Apartheid* religion which goes under the name of Christian Nationalism.

For the modern nationalist viewpoint on Christian Nationalism we turn to a very recent paper of Prof. C.W.H. Boshoff on this subject.[42] Boshoff begins by defining the term "nationalism," which nowadays, he says, has become unpopular because of the Nazi period in Hitler's Germany. He feels that it is unfair for people to judge South African Christian Nationalism by simply equating it with the kind of nationalism of Nazi Germany. According to Boshoff, Hitler was "remarkably unnationalistic." He was, rather, "chauvinistic-imperialistic."[43] And this had nothing to do with true nationalism.

Christian Nationalism did not develop in Germany but in Holland and in South Africa—in opposition to imperialism. "Christian" stands for adherence and obedience to Christ, who is the Lord of all, and obedience to Christ's Word; and "nationalism" signifies devotion to one's nation. (Boshoff prefers the word *Volk*.) Boshoff then goes on to define the *volk*. A *volk* is a people with common descent, with a common cultural heritage, and can express itself best "in its own state" (land).[44] Christian Nationalism thus, according to Boshoff, means devotion to a *volk* under the control of Christ. It is the way of life of a Christian people trying to live according to the Word of God in its national structures, in its economy, and in all its relationships.[45] The *volk*, says Boshoff, does not become deified, nor does it become the norm as was the case in Nazi Germany. The norm for the *volk* is always the Word of God: "Love the Lord your God with all your heart and your neighbor as yourself." This is, according to Boshoff, the central philosophy of Christian Nationalism.

From all this it should be clear, Boshoff contends, that Christian Nationalism is diametrically opposed to the *Herrenvolk* idea. It is also opposed to any form of world-escaping pietism and a pietistic interpretation of the Christian faith. The Christian *volk* has a responsibility toward the christianization of all cultures and its duty is "to grant the prosperity, happiness, and development which it desires for itself, to all peoples around it as well."[46] Here Boshoff echoes Dr. Malan, first National Party Prime Minister of South Africa and a Dutch Reformed minister, when he said:

The difference in colour is merely the physical manifestation of two irreconcilable ways of life; between barbarism and civilization, between heathenism and Christianity. . . . *Apartheid* is based on what the Afrikaner believes to be his divine privilege and calling—to convert the heathen to Christianity without obliterating his national identity.[47]

Christian Nationalism believes that God is the Supreme Ruler of church and state and he demands responsibility *to him alone* from church and political leaders. "Christian," Boshoff repeats, means following Christ in the sense of Col. 3:17, which reads: "And never say or do anything except in the name of the Lord Jesus, giving thanks to God the Father through him." In Christian Nationalism, according to Boshoff, there is no room for racial superiority or self-glorification, because at the center of its philosophy stands Matt. 7:12: "So always treat others as you would like them to treat you; that is the meaning of the law and the prophets."

For this reason, Boshoff concludes, the Afrikaner sees Christian Nationalism as "essential for the future, the peace, the liberation, and the prosperity of all peoples." Only one principle must apply to all situations: *Soli Deo Gloria!* (To the glory of God alone).[48]

It is hard to believe that Boshoff himself can believe all this. A mere recital of the existing *Apartheid* laws and practices in South Africa will make anybody wonder whether Boshoff is speaking of this country at all. But we must take Boshoff seriously, and we turn to a critique of Christian Nationalism by

another Afrikaner, Dr. André Hugo.[49] It is all the more im-
pressive because it comes from the heart of the Afrikaner
people. Hugo begins by voicing his sheer astonishment that a
nation which calls itself Christian would deem it necessary to
use such a term. This in itself, he says, shows that something is
wrong. He finds Christian Nationalism an impossible
combination—an "absolutely impermissable assimilation."[50]
Hugo points out that the term was first used in its contemporary South African meaning by Dr. Malan, already mentioned
above. At the same time another famous South African
theologian, Dr. Andrew Murray, had warned against using
such a term with the argument that "the danger exists that the
voice of blood, the voice of passion, of partisanship, of group
interest will overpower the voice of the gospel."[51] Dr. Murray
was not listened to and

today, after half a century of Christian Nationalism, we stand before
the terrifying reality of an Afrikaner nationalism which also controls
the religious life of the Afrikaner instead of the other way around.[52]

There were unmistakable signs that the church was being
more and more controlled by political ideology. According to
Hugo, the official church mouthpiece (*Die Kerkbode*) in-
creasingly became a channel for Nationalist Party prop-
aganda and people who protested against this state of affairs
were branded "liberals" and "disloyal." But the disloyalty
these people were accused of, Hugo writes

was not disloyalty to the gospel, it was disloyalty to the policy of the
State and the Church, in other words, *Apartheid*. In this way the
Church is being degraded to an important structure, necessary for the
ideology of the nation, exactly as in the times of the Deutsche
Christentum.[53]

At this point Hugo refers to the obviousness with which
church councils of the three Dutch Afrikaans churches have
ties with nationalistic and cultural organizations such as the
Federasie van Afrikaanse Kultuurverenigings (Federation of Afrikaans Culture), and he especially stressed the point that

probably 70 percent of the ministers of the three Afrikaans churches belonged to a secret nationalistic organization, the *Afrikaner Broederbond*. [54]

Against this background Hugo mentions two "alarming phenomena": The first is the extent to which human feeling and empathy have deadened within the Afrikaner, which he sees in the silence with regard to the "massive human suffering of the black community"; and the way criticism on government policy by other churches is branded "social gospel." The Dutch Reformed church, Hugo says, is seemingly convinced that it preaches "the pure gospel"; it is willing to give staggering amounts for missionary work;

yet in the meantime we are blind with regard to the misery of the people who live around us. . . . And this is the root of Christian Nationalism. Our thinking has become ethno-centric. [55]

The second phenomenon that concerns Hugo is what he calls the "aversion to anything 'not our own.' " This aversion manifests itself in a fearful isolationism and an almost neurotic fear of change. This influences what Hugo calls the "method and morality" of the Christian National State. Hugo concludes that these do not differ much from those of other regimes which may be termed "authoritarian." Indeed, Hugo considers the South African government to be totalitarian because "a small (white) minority rules with absolute and totalitarian powers over 22 million people." [56] "This is Christian Nationalism," Hugo concludes, "not in its ideal form, but in its true form, its practical execution in South Africa today." [57] Hugo's criticism of Christian Nationalism, uttered more than a decade ago, still applies today—even more so. Indeed, by their fruits ye shall know them.

In the light of this and of our knowledge of the true situation in South Africa today, it remains astonishing that Boshoff could have written what he did. Boshoff's use of biblical texts, like the *Landman Report*'s subsequent appeal to Christian ethics, is totally unacceptable, for these are not applied to the real situation or to the living experiences of people, but to a vague ideal. This is an attempt to alienate the Christian ethic from its context of liberation and subjugate it to the existing situation of oppression.

Christian Nationalism is an ideology alien to the Christian ethic. It is cruel and inhuman for it lives in terms of myths, "principles," grandiloquent ideals, and programs instead of in terms of human reality; and therefore it has no room for (or does not understand) human suffering.

It does not arise out of compassion and its program (i.e., the policy of *Apartheid*) does not stand the test of rational enquiry nor the searching light of reality. It fosters what Mannheim calls a "false consciousness," which takes on the form of an incorrect interpretation of one's own self; it tries to cover up one's real relations to others and the world and to falsify the facts of human existence by deifying, romanticizing, or idealizing them.[58]

Suffering under Christian Nationalism, blacks ask themselves with wonderment how the advocates of this system can so shamelessly quote biblical texts like Matt. 7:12 to undergird their philosophy. Again, this reveals not only the extent to which Christianity is whitenized in South Africa, but also the innocence which refuses to see, that innocence which must not be allowed to exist in the oppressor.

Black Christian Nationalism

Reverend Albert Cleage, Jr., pastor of the Shrine of the Black Madonna in Detroit, Michigan, takes a peculiar place among black theologians. His theological program is an instrument through which Cleage tries to rally black people around a nationalistic ideal. Important within the context of our discussion is the notion of a Black Christian Nationalism that Cleage advances.[59]

Cleage's Christian Nationalism is not based merely on political considerations; it is based on fundamental theological convictions. His theology begins and ends "with the historic fact that Jesus was a black man."[60] Cleage not only wants a separate political program for black people—black controlled economic, social, and political institutions; he wants a complete separation from white America, a "nation within the nation."[61] For blacks to believe in integration is "insanity," Cleage argues, for to dream of integration, one must first believe in the goodness of white people. Hence for Cleage integration is "the other side of black inferiority"[62] and Martin Luther King, working for integration, was a mystical kind of idealist who had no roots in objective reality.[63]

We have already alluded to the theological motif of Cleage's Black Christian Nationalism. Historically, Cleage maintains, the Jewish religion, and after that the Christian religion, were black religions. Christianity was originally the religion of a small tribe of nomads who were taken as slaves by ruthless white men. These slaves were descendants of the Black Jewish people—the Nation of Israel.[64] According to Cleage it is impossible that Israel, as we encounter it in the Bible, could have been "a white people." What biblical history tells us about Israel, therefore, is about the history of a black people: "Abraham was very closely identified with the black people of Africa." The Jews, in their wanderings to Europe and Russia, converted white people there to Judaism. The Jews who remained in that part of the world where black people are dominant remained black. And it was into this black nation that Jesus came, "born to Mary, a Jew of the Black tribe of Judah, a black people. . . . Jesus was a Black Messiah born to a black woman."[65]

Thus Cleage's theology is determined by his belief that Jesus was the black leader of a black people struggling for national liberation against the rule of a white nation, Rome.[66] Therefore, one can describe Cleage's theology as a black nationalistic, revolutionary theology. Within this framework, Cleage deals honestly and boldly with theological issues.

Consider for example the story of the Good Samaritan. The Samaritans, says Cleage, were Jews, a lost tribe, despised because they rejected the temple in Jerusalem. Jesus, however, considered them part of the nation that should be saved. Therefore, "the parable of the Good Samaritan was merely an effort to show Israel that these people could no longer be despised."[67] The point is made: Every black brother and sister must be saved and brought into the nation. This is also Cleage's practical program. Every black person belongs to the "chosen," the Black Nation, and every effort must be made to gather them into the Nation.[68] Cleage tells his congregation that a complete interpretation of the Christian faith is necessary, for "almost everything you were taught about Christianity was wrong."[69] Cleage accepts only the Old Testament and the three synoptic gospels.

Christians, he contends, have for many years misunderstood the teachings of Jesus. The ethic of the Sermon on the Mount—turn the other cheek, walk the second mile—is an *internal*, tribal ethic for the Black Nation. For Jesus, the whole idea of brotherhood and love had to do with love *within* the Black Nation. The Nation was in the process of being consolidated, called from their sense of identification with the white oppressor. Now they must learn to accept the fact that their power lay in their unity, in their willingness to forgive each other and to love, work, and struggle together. What Jesus said was meant only for the Black Nation.[70]

Still, according to Cleage, Jesus had to talk to the Nation in a special way, and they had to learn to adopt a new attitude, a new lifestyle. In this way, Jesus was really creating a completely new nation. This is also the revolutionary element in his work: To weak and oppressed people he talked about the transforming and redemptive power of love within the Nation. Thus it is that Cleage can say:

If a Black brother strikes you on one cheek, turn to him the other cheek, because we must save every Black brother for the Nation if we are to survive. . . . This is what Jesus was talking about. Turn the other cheek, go the second mile, go a hundred miles if necessary, if in this way you can save a Black brother.[71]

It is inevitable that this theological stance must have consequences for the ethic Cleage wants to follow. Cleage himself is explicit: The first step in Christian life is to know that there is an enemy. And "the man who helps you forget [that there is an enemy] is your worst enemy. That is the white man who pretends to be your friend."[72] Of course white people (*good* white people do not exist) are not only the enemy; they are also outside the Nation. That means that the commandments of Jesus do not apply to them. To love the oppressor, Cleage asserts, and to persuade him to love you "is certainly the acceptance of inferiority":

Nobody can love everybody. The white man does not love you. . . . You have less reason to love him than he has to love you. . . . [To love the enemy] is ridiculous. We have to concern ourselves with justice, not love. We can't go to the white man and ask him to love us. . . . It's futile. We want justice, and we are going to fight for justice. . . . Love is only something for inside the Nation.[73]

Much of what has been said with regard to "the religion" of Black Power and with regard to Christian Nationalism is applicable to Cleage. We do not want to underestimate the value of what Cleage is trying to do, creating a new Christian consciousness which, in contrast with what the black church in America has been doing generally for decades, tries to engage the church actively in the realm of politics and social responsibility. But we must reiterate that Cleage's total identification of the gospel with his particular brand of Christian Nationalism is totally unacceptable.

What Cleage says about the "national religion" of black people and its history may very well be true. But he expects us to believe this without the benefits of serious scientific analysis.[74] Although it can be argued that Cleage's theological position is merely the fruit of the alliances Christian theology has made with nationalistic ideologies, so that it is a case of "the chickens coming home to roost," we must deal with Cleage more seriously.

Cleage claims God solely for the black people, a conception which of necessity requires a national God, something we have also encountered when we dealt with white Christian Nationalism. This conception of God is denied by both the Old and New Testaments. God will neither allow himself to be claimed by any one people, nor will he be reduced to a mere symbol of their nationalistic aspirations.

The New Testament makes it abundantly clear that God in Christ has transcended all national, racial, and cultural barriers to gather his people into a new *koinonia.* Cleage's nationalistic ethic forces Yahweh into the form of a tribal God who, confined to the will of the nation he represents, endorses all the nation wants to do and condemns everyone not within that nation. In spite of the valid elements in Cleage's argumentation, we must conclude that Cleage's theology denies the very nature of the Christian church. And besides, a church which so identifies itself with a nationalistic ideology or a particular political program *has* to lose its essential character. When this happens, what then is the true meaning of the presence of the church in a society?

The concept of the Black Messiah and the relationship between love and justice we have already discussed. We affirm with Cleage the reality of the Black Messiah; the Christ of the slavemaster is not an adequate Christ for freed black people who affirm their dignity and freedom as children of God:

The black man has in the Black Messiah a Saviour. He discovers his own dignity and pride in a self-awareness that is rooted in black consciousness. Christ conceived in a black image is one of us and in a real sense he becomes our Lord and our God.[75]

At the same time, however, we reiterate that the literal skin color of the historical Jesus is of less theological significance than Cleage wants to admit. But Cleage must do this in order to maintain his theological exclusivism and his theory of the genetical predestination of the black people as the chosen people of God—the Black Nation. In this, he again has his counterpart in white Christian Nationalism with its belief in the "white chosen."[76]

We fear that Cleage's Black Christian Nationalism, however well intended, cannot and will not escape the fate of all quasi-religious nationalism. His concept of an "ethic for the nation only" is disturbingly reminiscent of the "for the *Volk* only" theology black South Africans must reject. In Cleage's theology there is no critical distance between the gospel and the ideology of the Black Nation, between the will of God and the desires of the Nation. Not the Torah and the Prophets, but Black Christian Nationalism has the final word, and Yahweh may merely function as an instrument.

It is ironic that among black theologians Cleage has but a few followers on this point. Rather, Cleage's ideas are coincidental with those who are the outspoken enemies of Black Theology: white South African Christian Nationalistic theologians. We for our part can no more accept Black Christian Nationalism than we can accept the Afrikaner's white, Christian National- ism, and blacks would do well to ponder the histories of these unholy alliances.

BLACK THEOLOGY AND IDEOLOGY

Christian faith transcends all ideologies and all nationalistic ideals. It transcends specific groups and nations with their specific ideals and interests. That is to say, to have political ideals is not in itself sinful; to identify them with the gospel of Jesus Christ is.

Christian faith is more than a mere alternative for ideology, in the sense that it is not merely a utopia (Mannheim). It is eschatological, rooted in the promises of Christ and the liberat- ing deeds of Yahweh and in the knowledge that these prom- ises, in a real sense, have had their fulfilment in Jesus Christ. Faith continually tests programs by the criteria of the gospel of Jesus Christ, discerning where they serve liberation, justice, and the wholeness of life within every situation.

This is the calling of Black Theology within the context of the black experience. The dangers along this road are evident, but liberation theology takes the risk of faith and believes that the point is not to move away from the situation or to try to stand esoterically above the situation as white theology thought it could do. Rather, Black Theology should continue to cultivate self-critical reflection under the Word of God within the situa- tion of blackness.

Black Theology must ask whether the actions of blacks for gaining their liberation are in accord with the divine will of

God, a thing that can be done only if the Word of God retains its critical and fulfilling function vis-à-vis all human activity. In this regard Gollwitzer offers a valid criticism of Cone's earlier theology.[77] He asks whether Cone does not too easily claim God's approval for any method the oppressed wish to choose to effect their liberation. Cone's "by any means necessary" ethic makes it difficult to deny this. We don't agree with Gollwitzer, however, when he states that Cone (and Black Theology) makes "selective use" of the Bible when he maintains the basic truth that the gospel *is* liberation. Gollwitzer considers the cross and the resurrection apart from the liberation-event.[78] This Black Theology refuses to do. Exodus and resurrection, cross and liberation are not disparate entities, but are caught up in the same liberation movement, represent the same divine reality effected by the same liberating God.

Black Theology seeks to interpret the world-wide revolution against inhumanity, exploitation, and oppression in which Black people have played a major role. In contrast to ideologies of power and white theology's alliances with them, the task of Black Theology is that of the Old Testament prophets as described by Labuschagne:

The prophets were not confronted with individual sinners, but with the ideology of the nation whereby they were brought into conflict, not with individuals, but with a whole nation. The generality and radicality of their judgment must be understood not only to originate in a profound consciousness of sin, but also in the realization that they were fighting an ideology which, like all ideologies, can never be reformed, but has to be radically and totally destroyed.[79]

CHAPTER FIVE

Beyond the Sorrow Songs

The Quest for a Black Ethic

*They that walked in darkness sang songs in the olden
days—Sorrow Songs—for they were weary at heart. . . .*

Frederick Douglass

*And the Lord answered me:
"Write down the vision;
make it plain upon tablets,
so he may run who reads it.
For still the vision awaits its time;
it hastens to the end—it will not lie.
If it seem slow, wait for it;
it will surely come, it will not delay.
Behold, he whose soul is not upright in him shall fail,
but the righteous shall live by his faith."*

Habakkuk 2:2-4

*In response to Bonhoeffer's question: "Who is Jesus Christ for us
today?" black theologians answer that he is black, by which they
mean that he identifies himself with the oppressed and seeks
their liberation. "Black" is therefore not primarily a racial
designation but a socio-political one.*

John de Gruchy

INTRODUCTION

In this last chapter we will once more investigate Black Theology, this time more specifically than we have until now, from a

socio-ethical perspective. Black Theology as a contextual theology is black people's attempt to come to terms with their situation. If blackness is indeed a life category that embraces the totality of the daily existence of blacks, it is logical that the black situation will, and must, determine partly the ethical stance blacks are to take in the world. Blackness must necessarily become a determining factor if Black Theology is to find an authentic black Christian ethic. For, as Manas Buthelezi has observed,

[Blackness] determined the circumstances of my growth as a child and the life possibilities open to me. It now determines where I live, worship, minister, and the range of my closest associates. . . . The totality of the only life I know has unfolded itself to me within the limits and range of black situational possibilities.[1]

The problem with traditional Christian ethics is not only that the black situation has never been taken into account, but that the ethic arrived at was based on a theology that did not in any way recognize the God of the oppressed. As a result, it was, to say the least, inadequately equipped to deal with the realities of oppression and liberation. It is now incumbent upon black people to search for new forms (new wine in new wine skins!) to express the liberation they experience in Christ through his deeds of liberation for them.

BLACK THEOLOGY, LIBERATION, AND OPPRESSION

The theology of James Cone persistently focussed on liberation as the content of Black Theology and the black Christian ethic. Black Theology is a theology of liberation because it arises from complete identification with the oppressed in their struggle, proclaiming that the struggle of the oppressed is God's struggle:

Black Theology is a theology of liberation because it is a theology which arises from an identification with the oppressed. . . . It believes that the liberation of black people *is* God's liberation.[2]

We have already alluded to Cone's contention that liberation and blackness go together. For Cone, we know now, blackness signifies oppression in *any* given society, and in order to know what God is doing in the world, one must know what Black Power is doing. God's revelation is black and all talk about liberation must be black talk. The liberation of the oppressed is a revolutionary activity; it means a radical break with the existing political and societal structures, a redefinition of black life along the lines of Black Power and self-determination.[3]

Liberation is liberation from white domination, making blacks free to define themselves and their own world. In this process, according to Cone, God chooses the side of the oppressed, works through them "by any means necessary."[4] Cone does not believe this "by any means necessary" ethic to be in opposition to the Christian love ethic. The message of love, he says, is still presented to blacks in white terms. God's love should never be considered separately from his righteousness and his liberating deeds:

Black Theology agrees that the idea of love is indispensable to the Christian view of God. The Exodus, the call of Israel into being as the people of the covenant, the gift of the Promised Land, the rise of prophecy, the Second Exodus and above all the incarnation reveal God's self-giving love to oppressed man.[5]

Because the love of God is a divine activity, to love the neighbor means to join God in his activity to liberate the oppressed.[6] God's love for blacks means that he has given them "somebodyness," the power to "become." By accepting the truth of this new image of themselves revealed in Jesus Christ, black people respond to God's love. To love whites, i.e., the enemy, is to confront them as a Thou without any intention of becoming an It.[7] The new black refuses to speak of love separated from justice and power, and profound love can only exist between equals.

In *A Black Theology of Liberation* Cone adds a new element: The love of God for people is revealed in God's willingness to become black. "He is black because He loves us, and He loves us because we are black."[8] Cone writes:

Black Theology cannot accept a view of God which does not present Him as being for blacks and *thus* against whites. Living in a world of white oppressors, black people have no time for a neutral God. The brutalities are too great and the pain too severe. . . . There is no use for a God who loves whites the *same as* blacks.[9]

This view of love (God loving whites the same as blacks) Cone calls "white." It is a love that tells blacks to walk the second mile and turn the other cheek. What is needed, according to Cone, is the divine love expressed in Black Power which is the power of black people to destroy their oppressors, here and now, by any means at their disposal.[10] This is why Cone can state that "love is not to accept whiteness," but rather "to make a decision against white people."[11] God's love is God's liberation of black people expressed in Black Power.

This of course, has consequences for Cone's ethic and his views on the issues of liberation and reconciliation. Cone believes that we cannot solve the ethical questions of the twentieth century by taking as example Jesus' actions from the first. We cannot follow in his steps. The question for the Christian is rather: What is God doing? Where is he at work? The question of violence is not the primary question for Cone. Black Theology does not overlook the fact that violence does exist,

[but] the Christian does not decide between violence and non-violence, evil and good. He decides between the less and the greater evil. . . . If the system is evil, then revolutionary violence is both justified and necessary.[12]

Besides, Cone argues—and we fully agree with him—white people with their sorry record of violence at every level are not morally equipped to preach the gospel of nonviolence to black people. The issue of violence gives rise to a further remarkable point. Although, on the one hand, Cone accepts that violence may be necessary and justified within the United States, on the other hand he is not convinced that "the American system is beyond redemption."[13] This while Cone knows that blacks are still oppressed even when they have achieved some economic and intellectual benefits. We shall return to this very interesting point.

As far as reconciliation is concerned, Cone is clear: Blacks cannot be reconciled on the terms of the very people who oppressed them and robbed them of their human dignity! It is impossible to talk about reconciliation until "full emancipation has become a reality for all black people" so that white people will address black people as black people.[14] Cone knows that reconciliation is "the work of God in which he becomes man in Jesus Christ," but this reconciling work of Christ involves a gathering of those who are committed to obedience in the world. Reconciliation is not only freedom from oppression; it is also freedom for God. That means being willing to do what God is doing: liberating the oppressed:

Because God's act for man involves liberation from bondage, man's response to God's grace of liberation is an act for his brothers and sisters who are oppressed.[15]

Consequently, there is a close relationship between reconciliation and liberation. Unless the hungry are fed, the sick are healed, and justice is given to the poor, there can be no reconciliation. This is why Cone believes that, just as for Jesus, reconciliation for man can be no easy, cheap thing. It is costly:

It is not joining hands and singing "black and white together" and "we shall overcome." Reconciliation means death, and only those who are prepared to die in the struggle for freedom will experience new life with God.[16]

On many points, J. R. Washington finds himself in agreement with Cone. For Washington, Black Theology as the "radical theology of Black Power" must take reconciliation seriously. He writes:

Indeed, reconciliation is not a thing of the past . . . but of the future black-white relations. But reconciliation . . . does not come on the other side of power; it comes on the other side of revolution and redemption. [17]

What Washington is saying is this: There is no other way for reconciliation to come but through revolution. Both are in his view equally inevitable. We have seen that for Washington a bloody revolution is the only solution to the race problem. Black Power, he says, is not faith in equality of power, nor in a balance of power, nor in a balance of error, nor even a balance of terror. The real task of Black Power is to "smash racism." [18] According to Washington, violence "in full force" is necessary to create this. Liberation toward the new society is liberation from white racism by any means necessary:

Violence is the only way to power for good. Every and any means is justified: if the end does not justify the means, nothing does. [19]

The new society that must be created in this way, according to Washington, is one of social justice with freedom and equality for all. Civil Rights is a failure because it operates within a system that produces racism, poverty, and disrespect for black people. The present failure of Black Power, according to Washington, is that it accepts this system "insofar as it permits black people to share in the decisions which are based on the perpetuation of racism and poverty." [20] The most important task of Black Power is to wipe out racism through revolution and so create the new humanity. "Following this venture, win, lose or draw, there will be a new America." [21]

Black Theology, Hope, and Reconciliation

It was not long before the ideas of Cone, Washington, and Cleage summoned reaction from other black theologians, who wished to offer new perspectives on Black Theology, to criticize or to applaud.

Preston Williams, in a critique of Cone's ethic, finds that Cone's point of departure is wrong. According to Williams,

Cone claims to know what God is doing in the world and, therefore, what people should do as agents of God.[22] But, says Williams, this knowledge that Cone claims to have is not derived from rational thinking about empirical facts; therefore to share Cone's conclusions about historical events one must simply accept on faith Cone's views on race, Scripture, and God's activity in the world "regardless of what one sees and hears to the contrary." The position of blacks in the United States at the present moment makes clear, Williams holds, that Cone's judgment on America is not correct, even though he agrees with Cone that racism "is endemic to white America."[23]

Williams also concedes that Cone is right in emphasizing liberation as the central theme of the Bible as witnessed in the Exodus, the proclamation of the prophets, and the message of Jesus. What is needed, however, is "a theological method that goes beyond stating what God is doing and grounds the justification for revolution in arguments which bind facts to belief in God."[24] Williams establishes a "fundamental contradiction" in Cone's theology:

Either one is loyal to the God who works on behalf of the oppressed of whom most happen to be black, or one is loyal to the blacks of whom some may be oppressed and some of whom may have a particular place in the plan of God for this day.[25]

What Williams is asking of Cone is "concrete facts" and rational discussions based on these facts. Williams offers an alternative which relies "upon beliefs and values associated with Christian faith and American constitutional principles."[26]

We admit that Williams, in speaking to the "contradiction" in Cone's theology, offers a sound point of criticism. Indeed in our opinion, Cone does have trouble keeping these two loyalties apart, and he goes far in identifying the aspirations of the oppressed unconditionally with the purposes of God. This also involves the issue of Cone's identification of blackness and oppression to which we shall return. Yet this statement of Williams reveals a fundamental difference in approach. For Cone, blackness signifies oppression, no matter what some blacks may have "achieved" in American society. For Williams however, what some blacks have been able to achieve makes a difference to his judgment on American society. That is why he says that Cone "is too prone to private interpretations of the black experience." Clearly Williams writes from another experience. It seems to us that Cone is speaking far more genuinely for blacks than Williams is able to do, especially for those blacks who are not so fortunate as to belong to the black middle-class society and whose position can be described by no other word than "oppressed."

At the same time, Williams's theological construction itself is not free from contradictions. He admits that liberation is the central theme of the biblical message and that "authentic Christianity affirms that God is on the side of the oppressed." Yet Williams reproaches Cone that by taking this stance he claims to know what God is doing in the world, implying that Cone is wrong. If Cone is right in saying that the gospel message is all about liberation (and Williams says he is), how else then can God's actions in the world be described but as liberating the oppressed? If the only way we can speak about God in the world of today is based on the testimony about him and his deeds of liberation in history, how else can we speak about him but as the God of the oppressed, wonderfully involved in history for the liberation of his children? What "facts" or "rational" deliberation does one need to be convinced of the will of God for the oppressed and the oppressor, other than the testimony about him and his divine activity in historical revelation? If this is so, what indeed are human beings to do if they want to be obedient to this God? Williams must choose: Either God is the God of the oppressed, working for their liberation and in Christ calling them to do his will, or he is not at all.

What then is the ethical "alternative" Williams offers which relies on "beliefs and values associated with Christian faith and American constitutional principles"? Whites, Williams says, should keep their promises. Black Americans, after all, are part of the "American Dream," and when the situation is altered, "lower-class blacks too, will leave the so-called lower class."[27] Ironically, Williams appeals to Martin Luther King, who himself has noted with explicit pleasure that black youth were most creative and revolutionary precisely when they had succeeded in discarding their middle-class values and ideas![28] King saw more clearly then than Williams does now that the American Constitution does not automatically spell freedom for blacks and that the "American Dream" is more easily dreamt (and believed in) on soft couches in middle-class suburbs than on hard board beds in black ghettos. Williams comes no further than asking for "reparations" so that "lower-class blacks" would be able to leave the "lower class" to become "middle-class" blacks. We contend that this "alternative" is no alternative at all, that it is not only based on "the American Constitution and Christian faith," but as we have said earlier on, also on a fundamentally different understanding of the black experience, which in its turn is based upon the old, rather thin-worn, dream of the "black bourgeoisie."

Another critic of Cone is J. Deotis Roberts, the author of *Liberation and Reconciliation: A Black Theology*.[29] As the title suggests, Roberts's critique focuses mostly on what he believes to be Cone's inability to successfully combine liberation and reconciliation in his theology. By his own admission, Roberts's ethics emerge out of his stand on the boundary between the view of "by any means necessary" on the one hand and the view that "ends and means are organically one" on the other.[30] Roberts admits a close relationship with the stance of Martin Luther King, who, according to him, had an ethic in which the right balance was found between love, power, and justice, an ethic "which will win in the long run."[31]

Roberts's thesis is that not only liberation, but liberation *and* reconciliation are the two main poles of Black Theology. He writes:

Liberation is revolutionary—for blacks it points to what *ought to be.* Black Christians desire radical and rapid change in America as a matter of survival. Black Theology is a theology of liberation. We believe that the Christian faith is avowedly revolutionary and, therefore, it may speak to this need with great force.[32]

By the same token Roberts regards reconciliation as crucial
and the ultimate post-revolutionary goal. At the heart of Black
Theology Roberts sees the question of "new wine in new wine
skins." Can the old relations, he asks, the old American institutions contain the new message of liberation and reconciliation? Reconciliation must happen between "equals."[33] At
the same time, however, Roberts still leaves room for "concerned white Christians" to do "charity work" (*sic!*) in the
black community.[34] Like liberation, reconciliation is not
"cheap" or "easy." It comes, Roberts claims, only after the
revolution, which in Roberts's thinking does not necessarily
mean a *violent* revolution. Reconciliation asks for sensitivity,
urgency, and obedient love. When love of God and love of
neighbor are intertwined, a radical obedience is achieved.
According to Roberts, blacks and whites have been living
inauthentic lives. The liberation Black Theology seeks is an
authentic Christian existence, understood by Roberts as a life
of "equity."[35]

Only through equity, this authentic existence, will reconciliation become a possibility. Liberation and reconciliation cannot be separated for "there is no shortcut to reconciliation that
does not pass through liberation, and there is no reconciliation
that does not include equity."[36]

Roberts proposes a Black Power based upon the Christian
ethic which must now move against institutional racism as
well as against individual racists. This ethic includes both
theological ethics (personal relationships) and social
relations.[37] What is needed, in Roberts's opinion, is a revolution, i.e., rapid social change. This process of change must
be undergirded by love, for "hate destroys the hater as much
as the hated":

A good reason for not becoming a black racist is to observe what
discrimination had done to the souls, minds and spirits of whites who
hate blacks. To hate someone at sight without ever getting to know
him is a form of sickness.[38]

Christians taking the Christian message seriously will regard reconciliation not only as a possibility but as the ultimate
end, knowing that we must be ready to forgive each other, just

as God forgives us because he loves us. Not only that, but there is always the experience of "tares and wheat." Roberts feels that this parable of Jesus is instructive for black/white relations. He observes:

Among both whites and blacks there is wheat and there are tares. Good and evil. It will be difficult to separate the two, even when we clearly recognize them, before "the time of the harvest." The human condition . . . is one in which there are imperfect strivings; therefore, being forgiven and forgiving others is a constant duty. [39]

We can agree with much of what Roberts says so far. But let us probe deeper into his social ethic. How precisely does he understand "new wine in new wine skins"? What does this mean in structural terms? The answer is somewhat surprising. Blacks now, Roberts confesses, "seek the good life, but on their own terms."[40] He therefore advises young blacks to study in order to "remove the barrier to the good life."[41]

Once more, we see a black theologian ask for nothing more than to get "into" the existing American structure. Roberts sees no need to criticize the system in depth. What he wants for blacks is "a better share." He pleads that the white Establishment should "hunt for better talent" in the black community so that the masses can benefit; this because of the fact that "as soon as blacks are relieved from the white Establishment the black Establishment attempts to take over."[42] His solution is to hunt for better talent. We cannot help but ask, better talent to do what? To even better exploit the poor? Roberts apparently fails to see that the masses cannot benefit precisely because the socio-economic structures that exist in America today are not created and maintained to serve these masses, and "new talent" to be still better agents of that system will not change the situation at all! A solution cannot be sought by imitating the American white capitalist system, or by creating a "better" kind of capitalism in the black community. What Roberts should ponder is a way in which blacks could really make a significant and fundamental contribution to the transformation of the system instead of a way of strengthening it by "getting in."

Roberts, after careful consideration, finds it extremely difficult to accept the "by any means necessary" ethic. He observes:

It may be applauded by black militants who have an ear for inflammatory rhetoric, but it will hardly do for a sound basis for Christian ethics in the area of race.[43]

Although it may be true that in American society hate and violence may be regarded the "most natural" response, Roberts urges blacks to press on to seek the "most Christian" response.[44]

In making a distinction between subtle, institutionalized violence and open, overt violence,[45] Roberts comes close, but not yet to the heart of the matter. Obviously influenced by Martin Luther King, Roberts views violence as impractical and purely destructive; it begets only hatred and more violence. In questioning the very practicality of the use of violence for social change, Roberts finds himself opposed to Cone:

Violence . . . is inconsistent with the Christian ethic. . . . There have been and are situations in the world in which violent revolution may be the lesser of two evils and the only path to liberation.[46]

But still Roberts is reluctant:

The history of such violent upheavals indicates that the masses seldom profit from the slaughter and injustice merely changes hands.[47]

Roberts is inclined to leave room for situations where violence is "unavoidable," and here he thinks of situations in Latin America and Southern Africa. He has, however, clear conditions for such situations. Should such an occasion arise, the violence used should be "programmed," it must be a means rather than an end, and it should only be used after better alternatives have been duly tried, as the lesser of two evils. This hesitation does Roberts credit and on this point his theological stance is much more authentic than that of both Cone and Washington. It is also laudable that Roberts, while living in the United States, does not lightly make violence "unavoidable" or "easy" for Christians in other parts of the world involved in the liberation struggle. But still there remains a question. Can violence ever be "programmed"? If violence, in the heat of the struggle, acquires this autonomy that we spoke of earlier, can one still make an intellectual decision on ends and means as Roberts wishes to do?

Roberts's concern for reconciliation does indeed offer a more secure basis for a black ethic than the "by any means necessary" philosophy. This is all the more significant because Roberts does not believe in "easy" reconciliation, but in a reconciliation which is inextricably bound to liberation. The Christian faith, he asserts, has never under any circumstances sanctioned a "by whatever means necessary" ethic: "We need to know how to decide and what to decide for. . . . We need to consider the relationship between motives, means and ends."[48] Black Theology must have an ethic inspired by Christian love which is always "love in action."[49] It is a love inspired by the Sermon on the Mount, seeking liberation and reconciliation with equity:

Our quest for a theological ethic must provide the ethical imperatives that will lead the church, black and white, to be the church—a liberating and reconciling church.[50]

Quite another line of thinking is offered by Major J. Jones.[51] Jones believes in nonviolence, criticizes Black Power, stumbles over the "strategic withdrawal" which Black Power finds so necessary because he holds onto the goal of integration. Separation by choice, he says, is as harmful as separation by force.[52] We want to respond to Jones immediately.

Jones apparently does not see that black people need this strategic withdrawal. Recovering one's personhood in a situation where one's very thinking has been perplexed by the thought patterns of the oppressor is difficult enough. To think that black people could do this "in the open" where even the most modest attempt could be smothered by the white power structure, to say nothing of the white liberal, is sheer wishful thinking. This withdrawal of black people from the direct and dominant influence of whites is necessary to gain the independence of thought and solidarity needed to counter the divide-and-rule policy of the oppressor. Moreover, if Jones does not know the difference between this separation and the forced separation of white power, how much has this to do with a tendency in Jones's thinking to give theological import to integration *as such*? The separation forced upon blacks by white power was (and still is) in the service of segregation and oppression. It is necessary in order to enable the white power structure to control even more effectively the minds and lives of black people. It is a separation controlled by white power. Black Power's call for strategic withdrawal serves to strengthen black people through consolidation and solidarity to break the hold of white power over them. It is a separation in the service of liberation. It is a separation in order to come back strong enough to claim what is rightfully one's own on one's own terms. This, it seems to us, is a significant difference.

Jones must understand once and for all that integration, which has been the ideal for so long, cannot be the primary interest of black people. At present, integration within any black/white context, whether in South Africa or in the United States, means "becoming white." This must be rejected. The ultimate goal for black people is liberation. This is the essential prerequisite for the structure of a new society. As such, integration is irrelevant. For black people who are politically powerless, economically exploited, and culturally deprived, the equitable distribution of decision-making power is of far more importance than physical proximity to white people. This does not mean that the alternative is *Apartheid*. Adam Small phrases it thus:

If, therefore, we reject Apartheid, it is for a much profounder reason, an infinitely profounder reason than that we want integration; we do not want integration, we reject it. We want to survive as men, and if we will not insist on our blackness we are not going to make it in a world peopled quite profusely with white nihilists, and especially not in a part of the world where we have to live with them, close to them, even in the midst of them.[53]

Jones equates Black Power with hatred and violence.[54] He believes that it is not possible for black people to learn love and respect for themselves without inevitably having to hate white people out of which, just as inevitably, flows violence. We have already spoken to the issue of self-love. Here we just wish to reiterate that black people do need to learn not to be ashamed of being black; they need to discover, as Martin Luther King said, "an unassailable and majestic sense of their own value." In doing this there is no necessity, let alone an inevitability, to hate the white person. Black self-love is black people "returning to normal"; it is the creative precondition for a new black/white relationship.

Jones defends nonviolence as the only possible Christian action,[55] and he strikes a point when he argues that "the self-defense adherents cannot escape the cogent question of who the master is," meaning that they cannot but respond *on the same level* as the white person who threatens them with violence.[56] Jones therefore pleads for nonviolence as (the only) Christian response, a response on a higher level, for then "the white man, traditionally having dealt with violence from all sides," would be taken by surprise:

The oppressor has not yet learned how to deal with nonviolence. He still does not know how to deal with a man who has the moral initiative of love on his side.[57]

The truth in this statement is undeniable. It would have helped, however, if Jones had taken the different forms of violence into account as both Roberts and Cone had done. Also, he does not see as clearly as Cone the violence inherent in the system of racism, nor does he make the distinction King made: hatred for the system while maintaining an active love for the person.

We also have difficulty following him sympathetically when he claims that "the real threats to freedom are those which come from within man himself."[58] In *Christian Ethics for Black Theology*, Jones reiterates this one-sided view:

To be liberated is to be conscious of the real self, and once a person finds the identity of the real self, once he knows who he is, . . . he will be a liberated and free person. . . . This is the liberation to which black Christian ethics calls all black people.[59]

Of course, one cannot deny that freedom, like power, begins within oneself. Within the oppressed there is a conditioned fear for freedom which has to be overcome; there is a decision for freedom to be made. Also we do not deny that it is possible to hold onto an essential inner freedom under the most degrading and inhuman conditions. But Jones's argument is quite another one. His is a mystical form of speech which under the present circumstances does not really speak to the need of black people. Jones offers a political pietism which totally ignores the threats to freedom from persons with whom and systems within which people have to live. Jones proposes an inner freedom which is designed to help black people "forget" black reality. Freedom is much more than just an *"innerweltliche"* experience; it is more than merely coming to terms with one's inner self. Freedom is also an objective reality.

Like other black theologians, Jones speaks of the necessity of a "revolution." For Jones this revolution is nonviolent and an expression of a theology of hope. The gospel itself is revolutionary. Jones explains: The simple fact of preaching the gospel is itself like putting sticks of dynamite into the social structure.[60] Jones wants to make clear what he means: A rebellion is to restore what is lost; a revolution is to create something new. This "new" is identified as an eschatological hope. Jones does not go further than this. Nowhere do his intentions become clear with regard to the kind of society Jones wants, except that he sees the end of racism and segregation as the ultimate goal. Black people must "make America what America must become"[61] and work for "a new day" which will come when black people will stand "as equal in the collective company of all God's children."[62] We shall return to this statement in the final part of this chapter.

Black Theology, Black Consciousness, and Liberation

We shall discuss Black Theology, Black Consciousness, and liberation *in South Africa* separately, for two reasons. First, the South African black theologians are mostly still defining the problems, and secondly one should acknowledge the different situations in South Africa and the U.S.A.

Black Theology and Black Consciousness are almost always mentioned simultaneously in South Africa. This is of special significance in the peculiar political and ecclesiastical situation in this country. Black Consciousness here means a decision toward and an act of solidarity, a *black* solidarity which encompasses all the different ethnic groups in the black community, sharing the solidarity of the oppressed. It is a positive, conscious determination to break down the walls erected by an *Apartheid*-inspired false consciousness between "coloureds," "Indians," and "Bantu." Black Theology seeks a community, a *black* community that cuts across all the artificial barriers of separateness, of *Apartheid*, of being-closer-to-white-peopleness that have, until now, so tragically divided them. It seeks a community of blackness, knowing that if black people do not become reconciled with themselves and with each other, nobody will be.

Blackness does not in the first place designate color of skin. It is a discovery, a state of mind, a conversion, an affirmation of being, which is power. It is an insight which has to do with wisdom and responsibility; for it is now incumbent upon black people to make South Africa a country in which both white and black may live in peace. "We have seen enough of white racism," writes Adam Small, "we have suffered enough from its meaning—we cannot want to be racist in our blackness."[63] This is an awesome responsibility and a task black people can take upon themselves only in the Name of the Lord, for in doing so they must somehow find the courage and the power to love white people (Baartman). This can be done only by the "real black people":

The real black people are those who embrace the positive description of "black" as opposed to "non-white," which is a definition in terms of others, not in terms of yourself. . . . This forces white people to recognize their whiteness and all its consequences.[64]

This is a profound statement of power. In a country where blackness is non-beingness, where black people have no rights, dignity, or self-respect, where an extremely refined system of laws shouts "inferiority" at the black person at every level—in such a situation blacks say with Small:

Our insight is the following: We will live without apology, or as if apologizing. . . . Whites have goaded and do goad us to humiliations which all add up to our believing that we live by their grace. Now we are rejecting that idea. . . . This has been the biggest impertinence on the part of whites, this idea that they hold life for us in their hands. Our movement towards our blackness means the realization, the clear realization that no one at all, no man, holds life in his hands for us. We are not beggars for life. . . . Protest will therefore play a role in our future actions but we will realize that protest is a kind of begging; but again, we cannot beg. Protest will be a secondary form of expression altogether. . . . The primary form of expression will be the manifestation of our blackness, time and time again—and again, whether whites will understand this or not will not be the point at all. We are not there for whites; we are there.[65]

It must be clear that this expression of Black Theology is not out to deproblematize the situation. Blacks do not look to "integration" as the "solution" to the problems of South African society, neither are they out to declare that God is "colorless"—not after what the white god has done. This brings us to Black Theology.

Almost at once we meet the call for a "re-examination of Christianity."[66] There is a strong resentment about the fact that the African religious heritage was constantly discarded as "heathenism" and "barbarism" while Christianity and western culture were indissolubly linked together under one divine cloak. The role of missionaries and missions is being critically reconsidered in the light of the black experience.

Black Theology here seeks a God who will not rest until his children are liberated and who will not permit a lie to exist unchallenged. It seeks a gospel relevant to the situation of the oppressed in South Africa. Blacks detest the way western theology has departmentalized life and forced upon the African mind its dualistic pattern of thinking—an element completely foreign to the biblical mentality and African traditional thought. Therefore, Black Theology proclaims the totality of

God's liberation and in the total liberation seeks the realization of the wholeness of life. This wholeness embraces the total existence of human life in the present; it embraces the total meaning of black *being* with regard to past, present, and future. For the South African black theologian, the confession that *Christ is black* is of profound existential import, for at present, writes D. D. L. Makhatini, Christ is still foreign:

He is an *Umlungu*—a white man. Instead of becoming one of us and with us, a brother, he becomes our *nkosana*, the "boss" himself. . . . To say Jesus is black . . . relieves us from *begging* him and encourages us to *ask* him to fulfil his promises concerning us. [67]

In calling for this actualization of the gospel for the black situation, Black Theology in South Africa is also an essential correction of traditional western theological thinking.

There is also a call for the church to go (back) to the roots of broken African community and tradition. It must examine why certain traditions were considered wholesome for the African community and whether these traditions can have a humanizing influence on contemporary society. Black Theology takes upon itself "to speak a word of hope to people without power":

And this word of hope cannot contain any promise that one day they will have power over others, even those others who oppress them now. It must be a hope that one day we will live together without masters or slaves. [68]

Bishop Zulu wrote a rather critical article on Black Theology. [69] He knows that "western civilization is basically selfish" and sees as the purpose of Black Theology to lead black people to see that when white people treat them as less human, when they exploit blacks, they are being unfaithful to the revelation of God in Christ. "The Christian God," he writes, "aims to set the black man free from the white man's fetters." Nonetheless, Zulu has some difficulty with those exponents of Black Theology "who give the impression that theology should be the handmaid of the black revolution and that this revolution necessarily should be violent."[70] Black theologians, he warns, should guard against equating God being on the side of the oppressed with the oppressed being on the side of God, and equating human love with God's love.

This criticism by Bishop Zulu has unfortunately been misused in a number of ways by white theologians for their own purposes. We must note, however, that Zulu's criticism of Black Theology is clearly uttered within the framework of his confirmation of the oppression and the need for liberation of blacks. He also notes that this liberation can be effected only by blacks themselves, and this warning, it seems to us, is given within the framework of solidarity in the struggle for liberation.[71]

To summarize: As far as I can determine, for most South African black theologians Black Consciousness is Black Theology (or very closely related). Black Consciousness implies "the awareness by black people of the power they wield as a group, economically and politically."[72] This is again the relation with Black Power. Black Theology calls upon black people to affirm this. It is not only concerned with internal bondage, but also with external enslavement. It is an awareness of "the failure of white theology to work selflessly towards the values and ethics Christianity claims to uphold."[73]

Black Theology in South Africa has not yet come forward with a specific social ethic. What follows in the next part of this chapter will be our endeavor to advance such an ethic for Black Theology.

TOWARD AN ETHIC OF LIBERATION

Christians should be engaged in historical action. They should, to the best of their ability, be doing the will of God, i.e., liberating the oppressed. What Christians do can only make sense within the framework of God's liberating deeds for those who look to him for their liberation. It stands to reason that Black Theology, as reflection on the praxis of liberation within the black situation, must have an ethic of liberation.

A Situational Ethic

Black Theology's situation is the situation of blackness. We have warned earlier that a contextual theology should remain critical and prophetic with regard to its own situational experience, because it is critical reflection under the Word of God. This means that the liberation praxis is finally judged not by the demands of the situation, but by the liberating gospel of Jesus Christ. The danger of a contextual theology being overruled by the situational experience and as a result succumbing to absolutistic claims is very real.

We fear that in this respect Cone's theology is particularly vulnerable. Cone claims, so we saw, God *solely* for the black experience. We submit that to make *black* as such *the* symbol of oppression and liberation in the world is to absolutize one's own situation. Black Theology, says C. Eric Lincoln in a critique on Cone,

is bound to the situation in this sense, that God's confrontation with white racism is but *one* aspect of God's action in a multi-dimensional complex of interaction between man and man, and God and man.[74]

Cone's mistake is that he has taken Black Theology out of the framework of the theology of liberation, thereby making his own situation (being black in America) and his own movement (liberation from white racism) the ultimate criterion for all theology. By doing this, Cone makes of a contextual theology a regional theology, which is not the same thing at all. Cone is certainly right in claiming that the only Christian expression of theology in the United States (and for that matter in South Africa) is Black Theology, inasmuch as the gospel is a gospel of liberation and Christian theology is therefore a theology of liberation, in our case black liberation to begin with. But in making this the ultimate criterion for all liberation theology, is Cone not wide open for an ideological takeover?

Moreover, if black is simply determinative for oppression and liberation everywhere and under any circumstances, if the only legitimate expression for liberation has to be black, does

Cone not close the door to other expressions of liberation theology? Can the Latin American theologian concede that the only way to recognize God's actions in history is "through the most radical deeds of Black Power"? Can, for instance, the American Indian liberation theology (God is Red!) share in this absolute claim of blackness?

Indeed, Black Theology is a theology of liberation in the situation of blackness. For blacks, it is the only legitimate way of theologizing—but *only within the framework of the theology of liberation.* Black Theology, therefore, finds itself in intention and theological methodology, and certainly in its passion for liberation, not only alongside African Theology, but also alongside the expressions of liberation theology in Latin America and Asia. And it is indeed in these expressions of Christian theology that western theology will ultimately find its salvation.

We have already pointed out that Black Theology speaks of "total liberation" in the same way that the African heritage speaks of the "wholeness of life." It focusses on the dependency of the oppressed and their liberation from dependency in all its dimensions—psychological, cultural, political, economical, and theological. It expresses the belief that because Christ's liberation has come, total human liberation can no longer be denied. It follows that this ethic is an ethic of liberation. Its character is situational, social, and eschatological. It does not, however, arise out of the situation, but in the situation.[75] The situation is never an entity *an sich* which autonomously determines the ethic of liberation. It has a history, and the results of the action within a given situation will have some bearing on its future. A black ethic will arise, therefore, in the black situation; it will be determined by the black experience in order to be authentic, but it will not be confined to the black experience, neither will black situational possibilities and impossibilities be its only determinant.

G. Th. Rothuizen has pointed out that a Christian ethic is of necessity a social ethic.[76] This is not to say that the personal dimension is negligible, but the authenticity of Christian ethics lies in its social awareness. Rothuizen goes even further. Not only must a Christian ethic be a social ethic, it must be a decidedly *political* ethic.[77] Jan Milic Lochman names the primary concerns of a Christian social ethic:

1. Objectively, the aim is to change inhuman conditions;
2. Subjectively, it is solidarity with the oppressed.[78]

We propose not only to change the sequence but also to add another dimension. The content of a Christian ethic is liberation. The first objective must be the identification of the human situation. Unless one knows that one is oppressed, unless one knows the oppressor, one cannot be liberated. This process of identification has to do with (re)education of the people and the discovery of one's own negative involvement leading to positive engagement.

Secondly, within the black situation solidarity with the oppressed becomes active engagement for liberation, leading, thirdly, to the transformation of oppressing and inhuman structures. Black Theology knows that the biblical message of God's liberation has historical as well as eschatological dimensions. It does not only rest upon the historical event of the Exodus, but it also points to the future, the future of Yahweh which he has made also the future of his people. This eschatological dimension should not lead to a theological paralysis as has so often been the case in theology, a waiting-patiently-upon-the-Lord kind of attitude, an attitude which leads to a disease Martin Luther King called "giveupitis."[79]

Nor must it lead to a theological escapism, an other-worldly religiosity which for so long has been a favorite way out for blacks. Black Theology realizes that New Testament eschatology is a call to arms, a summons not to be content with the existing situation of oppression, but to take sides with the oppressed and the poor and subsequently for the new humanity and the new world (Rom. 6:4, 12:2).

Black Theology agrees fully with Rasker on this point:

This is to say that such an eschatological ethic would dissociate itself from an "ethic of ordinances" (Ethik der Ordnungen) and would take on the character of an ethic of transformation.[80]

This transformation of society can be called a revolution and this revolution need not necessarily be violent. We understand such a revolution to be a fundamental social change. It is a transformation, a movement from what is to what *ought to be*. For Christians can never acquiesce in the status quo, but they continually challenge the structures of society where they fall short of the fullness revealed in Christ.

Love, Liberation, and Justice

Black Theology takes Christian love very seriously.[81] Because love stands at the very center of Yahweh's liberating acts for his people, any interpretation of Christian love that makes of it an ineffective sentimentality must be rejected. We agree with King and Cone that it is impossible to separate love from justice and power. Love is always love in righteousness. In speaking of righteousness we do not mean the forensic righteousness in the Pauline sense of the word, but the kingly justice whereof Jesus speaks. For when Jesus speaks of the "poor" and the "poor in spirit" and of the righteousness that shall be given them, he speaks of those who are socially oppressed, those who suffer from the power of injustice, those who depend upon Yahweh for their liberation. Ridderbos has conclusively shown that Jesus did indeed mean this kingly justice in the Old Testament sense and meaning. He writes:

The poor . . . look forward to God's liberation of his people from the power of oppression and injustice that is continued for the present. *And it is this longing for liberation which is indicated as "hunger and thirst after righteousness" in the Beatitudes in Matthew.* . . . It must not be understood in the Pauline sense of imputed, forensic righteousness, but as the kingly justice which will be brought to light one day for the salvation of the oppressed and the outcasts. . . . It is *this* justice which the poor and the meek look forward to in the Sermon on the Mount.[82]

Speaking of God's love without his righteousness betrays an oppression-mindedness Black Theology cannot tolerate. Cone is correct when he asserts that righteousness is that side of God's love which expresses itself through black liberation.

We cannot accept, however, Cone's contention that "to love is to make a decision against white people." We would have thought that to be able to love white people would mean precisely to make a decision *for* them! For their humanity, however obscure, against their inhumanity, however blatant. For their liberation, and against their imprisonment of themselves. For their freedom, against their fear; for their human authenticity against their terrible estrangement.

Reading Cone, one sometimes cannot help feeling that Zulu was right to warn against equating God's love with our human understanding of love and against the identification of "God being on the side of the oppressed with the oppressed being on the side of God." By the same token we cannot accept Washington's glib assertion: "The enemy may not love the violent aggressor, but he certainly respects him."[83] In reality this is not love Washington is speaking about, nor respect, but fear. And fear has very little to do with respect. In taking this stand, Washington makes fear the basis for human relations, and he advances the very thing he says that Black Power is not: a balance of terror.[84]

Liberation theology reclaims the Christian heritage and reinterprets the gospel to place it within its authentic perspective, namely, that of liberation. In so doing, it questions the historical role of the Christian church, the alliances of the church with "the powers that be" and insists on a true church, i.e., a church that proclaims and lives by the liberating gospel of Jesus Christ. In other words, in this regard Cone is right: One cannot speak of a Christian, segregated church. Liberation theology seeks a church that ministers to the poor not merely with a sense of compassion but with a sense of justice. This means that the church ought to discover that the state of poverty and oppression is ugly, impermissible, and unnecessary; that conditions of poverty and underdevelopment are not metaphysical but structural and historically explicable. In other words, poverty is one side of a coin of which the other side is affluence and exploitation. The church must discover that oppressed people are not merely unconnected individuals but a class.

A theology and an ethic thus engaged accept theology not

merely in terms of what it says, but in terms of what it is doing for the oppressed. It presses for active engagement of the church in socio-political affairs in its search for the truth which shall make free. We must be clear about this: The quest is for a church that dares to be the *church,* that dares to take upon itself, as did its Lord, to side with the poor and the downtrodden and to liberate the oppressed. The truth thus uncovered and translated into action by the church is not a description of reality but an involvement in reality, just as faith is active engagement in obedience to God, "the action of love within history," as Assmann says. The ethic of Black Theology, therefore, is an ethic of liberation. As such it is an ethic of transformation and not merely of survival.

Challenging the internal as well as the external dependency of black people, the change it calls for is a *qualitative* change. It is our contention that black theologians have not yet taken this aspect seriously. We have found that ultimately Roberts's goal for blacks is to share in "the good life," by which he means the kind of life American society offers the privileged. Preston Williams wants white Americans to keep their promises so that black Americans may also share in the "American Dream" and so that "lower-class blacks" may become "middle-class blacks." Major Jones and Joseph R. Washington, as we have seen, want "equality" through "rapid change," "revolution"—violent revolution being the only alternative for Washington. Nowhere, however, have we found a social ethic that satisfies us.

Fundamental to this, it seems, is the reasoning that racism is the only demon blacks have to fight. "Any analysis that fails to deal with racism, that demon embedded in white folks' being, is *ipso facto* inadequate."[85] While absolutely not minimizing racism as a demonic, pseudo-religious ideology (who, coming from South Africa, can?) we must nonetheless ask: Is racism indeed the only *issue?* It seems to us that there is a far deeper malady in the American and South African societies that manifests itself in the form of racism. The deepest motivation of the Portuguese in Southern Africa was not racism. Nor is racism the deepest motivation of the economic colonialism of the

United States in Latin America, or of the multinationals all over the "Third World."

And even in South Africa there are signs that should circumstances but allow, some whites would be quite willing to replace the insecurity of institutional racism with the false security of the "black bourgeoisie." In this, black theologians still fail to see what was seen by Martin Luther King and Malcom X: the relation between racism and capitalism, evident not only in the oppression of blacks in the United States itself, but also in the political and economic relationship supported by the United States (and other rich countries) between rich and poor nations.[86] Let us for the moment focus on James Cone, who writes:

> We will not let whitey cool this one with his pious love-ethic, but will seek to enhance our hostility, bringing it to its full manifestation. Black survival is at stake here, and black people must define and assert the conditions.[87]

This may sound fine, so far as it goes. But what does Cone have in mind? It is not enough to speak only of survival, as Cone repeatedly does. In a deep sense this seems to suggest a certain hopelessness, just "making it," "just getting by." Black Theology is a theology of survival, says Cone. We contend that it is more than that. If Black Theology is only to be understood in terms of the mere survival of black people, black liberation will never become a reality. If indeed black people now live beyond the Sorrow Songs, if indeed they are determined to define their own future, then one cannot speak merely of "survival."

Cone knows, better than Williams for example, that all is not well in America. Even when blacks have some economic and intellectual power, he still considers them "oppressed."[88] His answer to this situation is "revolution." A radical revolutionary confrontation. What does Cone mean by "revolution"?

> Revolution is everything that rejects the "holy ordinances" of the past, i.e., which questions the domination of the white oppressor.[89]

In black/white terms, Cone's revolution means a refusal to accept white definitions, white values, white limitations—any kind of white domination or black dependency. This refusal may have a violent character. It forms the process of liberation for blacks "by any means necessary." This liberation is, as Cone says, not only liberation *from*, but also liberation *to*. What does Cone have in mind? We get a clue when Cone admits that reconciliation is only possible between "equals." So equality is what Cone is after, but he lacks, it seems to us, a sound social critique, a critique of ideology and hence he lacks the sensitivity to define precisely and constructively this "equality."

Frederick Herzog puts the cogent question to James Cone. "What is the meaning of 'equality' in this society?"[90] Indeed that is the question. Reconciliation requires a new image of humanity which is why reconciliation without liberation is impossible. But the new image of humanity requires new structures in society—new wine in new wineskins! How new, then, are black persons who move out of their old lives of poverty and dejection into a higher status in the unchanged structures of an oppressive and exploitative system? In other words, the question really is, how do black theologians define liberation?

In defining the black American situation Cone is undoubtedly brilliant. But if he cannot go beyond that, his analysis will become nothing more than an emotional catharsis for blacks and a spiritual masochistic experience for whites —nothing new in the black/white relationship. Because Cone ultimately leaves the American capitalistic system intact, a further question of Herzog is to the point. Can Cone guarantee, Herzog asks, that his theology will not become a justification for a black bourgeoisie, indeed, servant to it, and whether Black Theology can really offer America an alternative for the present "way of life."[91]

When Cone tries to answer Herzog, he does not answer him at all. The question still remains: not whether blacks want to be equal to whites, but whether they want to be equals in this particular system this society adheres to. To our mind that would mean becoming equal partners in exploitation and de-

struction. Surely one must see that "getting into" the main-
stream of American society would not really solve the problem
at all. American exploitation and oppression do not begin and
end with black people (in the U.S.) only! And the dependency
of black people would not be broken by "joining whites."
Black Theology, as an integral part of the theology of liberation
realizes this and in its ethic seeks solidarity (true solidarity!)
with oppressed people all over the world. In this way it will
become clear that racism is but one incidental dimension of
oppression against which the total struggle should be waged.

Cone ends his article in *Evangelische Theologie* with this
rather revealing sentence: "We've got to make the best of a bad
situation."[92] This may be survival, but it certainly is not liberation, and we fear that here an ethic of survival might just
become an Establishment ethic. If this is indeed Cone's last
word, then what he offers as an "ethic of revolution" will not
be much more than a sort of "revolutionary revivalism."

Black Theology, then, must mean a search for a totally new
social order, and in this search it will have to drink deep from
the well of African tradition, to use what is good and wholesome for contemporary society. Blacks should not be dis-
couraged by those who deem this effort "utopian," for all
through black history black people have lived through their
strong belief in that "land beyond Jordan," in that reality
which is there, beyond the whip and the slavemaster, beyond
the poverty and dejection, leaving black children a legacy of
hope. Blacks who know of the liberation in Jesus Christ, the
Black Messiah, no longer walk in darkness; they live beyond
the Sorrow Songs. In the words of Rubem Alves:

This "utopianism" is not a belief in the possibility of a perfect society,
but rather a belief in the nonnecessity of this imperfect order. Christian utopianism is based on the vision that all social systems are under
God's historical judgment.[93]

In breaking away from the old oppressive structures of our
society, seeking new possibilities, creating room for the realization of true humanity, Black Theology seeks the true pur-

pose of life for blacks as well as whites. Blacks want to share with white people the dreams and hopes for a new future, a future in which it must never again be necessary to make of Christian theology an ideology or part of a particular aggressive cultural imperialism. Black Theology, by offering a new way of theologizing, desires to be helpful in discovering the truth about black and white people, about their past and present, about God's will for them in their common world.

Black Theology sincerely believes that it is possible to recapture what was sacred in the African community long before white people came—solidarity, respect for life, humanity, and community. It must be possible not only to recapture it, but to enhance it and bring it to full fruition in contemporary society. Genuine community lies beyond much struggle and despair, beyond reconciliation which will not come without conflict. It will come only through faith and courage. For blacks, this is the courage to be black. But again, this need be no otherworldly dream; it is as real as Africa itself. Indeed, *Motho ke motho ka batho babang*. This age-old African proverb has its equivalent in almost all African languages, and its meaning is still as profound as ever; even more so: One is only human because of others, with others, for others. This is Black Theology. It is authentic; it is worthwhile. It is, in the most profound sense of the word, gospel truth.

NOTES

Introduction

1. James H. Cone, *Black Theology and Black Power* (New York, 1969), p. 1.

2. *NCBC Statement on Black Theology*, 1976.

3. Rollo May, *Power and Innocence* (New York, 1972).

4. Ibid., p. 48.

5. Ibid., p. 49.

6. Ibid., p. 50.

7. Ibid.

8. "Western Christian civilization" is regarded as one of the pillars on which *Apartheid* stands. Cf. N.J. Rhoodie and H. Venter, *Apartheid* (Pretoria-Cape Town, 1960), p. 30.

9. G.T. Rothuizen spoke very aptly to this point in a commentary on Ps. 142:5: "This seems almost the worst that can happen to anyone: that no one wants to help him. Only one thing seems to me to be even worse—that nobody wants to be helped by him. This is the worst of South Africa: Not that whites do not want to help blacks, but that they do not want to be helped by blacks" (G.T. Rothuizen, *Landschap, Een bundel gedachten over de Psalmen* [Kampen, 1968], 3:261–62).

10. For an excellent and thorough discussion of this problem, cf. H. Achterhuis, *De Uitgestelde Revolutie, Over Ontwikkeling en Apartheid* (Baarn, 1973).

11. D. Crafford, "Die Moderne Kruistog teen Suid Afrika," in *Die Kerkbode* (Cape Town), January 6, 1971.

12. *Hansard*, no. 17, June 4, 1975, col. 7367 (Cape Town, 1975).

13. Cited in Major J. Jones, *Black Awareness* (Nashville, 1971), p. 26.

Chapter One

1. James Cone, *A Black Theology of Liberation* (New York, 1970), p. 17.

2. Gustavo Gutiérrez, *A Theology of Liberation* (New York, 1973), pp. 7–15.

3. Ibid., p. 11.

4. Cone, *Black Theology*, p. 45.

5. Hugo Assmann, "El aporte cristiano al proceso de liberación de América Latina" (The Christian Contribution to the Process of Liberation in Latin America). Paper presented at a meeting of ISAL, Ñaña, Peru, 1971. This essay is included in Assmann, *Theology for a Nomad Church* (Maryknoll, New York, 1976), pp. 129–45.

6. *Theology in Action*, Workshop Report of the East Asia Christian Conference (Tokyo-Perth, 1973).

7. Cf. Cone's discussion of the black experience and Scripture, in *The God of the Oppressed* (New York, 1975).

8. *Theology in Action*, p. 19.

9. Cf. Rothuizen, *Wat is theologie? Bonhoeffers laatste woord tot zijn studenien*, Kamper Cahier no. 13 (Kampen, 1970), p. 12.

10. Gutiérrez, *Theology of Liberation*, p. 12.

11. Cf. the ecumenical discussion on this subject in *Ministry in Context*, T.E.F. Booklet (London, 1972); *Learning in Context*, T.E.F. (London, 1973); *Viability in Context*, T.E.F. (London, 1975); also Daniel von Allmen, "The Birth of Theology," in *International Review of Mission* (January 1975), pp. 37–51.

12. Cf. the response of white South African Dutch Reformed theologians to Black Theology in *N.G.T.T.*, January 1973.

13. *Theology in Action*, p. 19.

14. Ibid.

15. Statement by the NCBC issued June 13, 1969, in Atlanta, Ga.

16. Cf. e.g. M.M. Thomas, *The Christian Response to the Asian Revolution* (London, 1965); idem, "Issues Concerning Life and Work of the Church in a Revolutionary World," in A.H. van den Heuvel, ed., *Unity of Mankind*, W.C.C. (Geneva, 1969), pp. 89–98.

17. Cone, *A Black Theology of Liberation*, p. 17.

18. Ibid., p. 28.

19. Ibid., p. 12.

20. Cf. F.C. Fensham, *Exodus*, in the series *De Prediking van het Oude Testament* (Nijkerk, 1970), pp. 23–26.

21. Cf. C. van Leeuwen, "Bevrijding in het Oude Testament," in *Rondom het Woord* (Kampen, 1974), p. 1.

22. There is general agreement among Old Testament scholars about this, even if there is some difference of opinion on what is called "The Song of Moses" and "The Song of Miriam"—the latter being

regarded as more ancient than the first. This does not change the fact, however, that we have here an authentic, ancient text of tremendous importance in the history and religious life of Israel. J.P. Hyatt calls vv. 1–12 "very old" (*Exodus,* New Century Bible, pp. 162–63). Cf. further among many titles on the topic: J. Bright, *A History of Israel* (London, 1966); H. Berkhof, *Christus de zin der geschiedenis* (Nijkerk, 1966); Y. Kaufmann, *The Religion of Israel,* (Chicago, 1969); G. Fohrer, *Das Alte Testament,* I (Gutersloh, 1969). H. Gressmann says in this regard: "Even the radical critics must concede that this song could only have come 'out of the situation.' This song is from the time of Moses" (Cited in M. Buber, *Schriften zur Bibel* [Munich, 1964], 2:86.

23. Cf. van Leeuwen, "Bevrijding," p. 7.

24. Cf. G. te Stroete, *Exodus,* in the series *De Boeken van het Oude Testament* (Roermond, 1966), pp. 17ff. Also J.M. de Jong, "De Opstanding van Christus," in C. Dippel, *Geloof en Natuurwetenschap* (Den Haag, 1967).

25. Cf. B. van der Merwe, *Pentateuchtradisies in die Prediking van Deuterojesaja* (Groningen, 1956); D. Daube, *The Exodus Pattern in the Bible* (London, 1963); W. Zimmerli, "Der Neue Exodus in der Verkundigung der beiden grossen Exilspropheten," in *Gottes Offenbarung,* series *Theologische Bücherei* 19 (Munich, 1963), pp. 197ff; C. van Leeuwen, "Bevrijding," p. 6; also Gutiérrez, *Theology of Liberation,* pp. 155ff.

26. Cf. Gutiérrez, *Theology of Liberation,* p. 156; also Zimmerli, "Neue Exodus."

27. Cf. C.J. Labuschagne, "De Godsdienst van Israel en de andere godsdienstein," in *Wereld en Zending, Tijdschrift voor Missiologie,* no. 1, 1975; M. Buber, "Gericht über die Richter," in *Schriften,* pp. 964–70.

28. Cf. J. Verkuyl, *De Boodschap der Bevrijding in deze tijd* (Kampen, 1970), p. 23.

29. Cf. Gutiérrez, *Theology of Liberation,* p. 167; also H.N. Ridderbos, *The Coming of the Kingdom* (Philadelphia, 1962) [Dutch: *De Komst van het Koninkrijk,* Kampen, 1972], passim.

30. Cf. H.D.A. Major, T.W. Manson, and C.J. Wright, *The Mission and Message of Jesus* (New York, 1947); William Barclay, *Jesus as They Saw Him* (London, 1963); J. Arthur Baird, *The Justice of God in the Teaching of Jesus* (London, 1963)—who all ignore this crucial passage completely. Cf. also K.H. Rengstorf, *Das Evangelium Lukas, das N.T. Deutsch* (Göttingen, 1969).

31. So especially William Manson, *Luke,* in series *Moffat N.T. Commentary* (London, 1930); D.A. Schlatter, *Das Evangelium Lukas*

(Stuttgart, 1931); E. Earle Ellis, *The Gospel of Luke, New Century Bible* (London, 1966); H.J. Degenhardt, *Lukas, Evangelist der Armen* (Stuttgart, 1964), give no attention to this passage. In the same vein as Manson we hear Norval Geldenhuys, who devotes a long passage to the question whether Jesus had read the text in Hebrew or Aramaic! N. Geldenhuys, *The Gospel of Luke,* in the series *The New London Commentary,* 7th ed. (London, 1969). It is strange that this same breed of theologians does not hesitate for one moment to accept the wonders of Jesus (wherein this same truth is demonstrated) as authentic gospel material and as historical truth.

32. Cf. his argumentation in "Die Mitte der Zeit" (Tübingen, 1962) pp. 29ff.

33. G.N. Stanton, *Jesus of Nazareth in New Testament Preaching,* (London, 1973), p. 66. For further examination of Conzelmann's method, cf. pp. 56ff. Stanton does a brilliant investigation of this gospel material in an essay, "On the Christology of Q," in *Christ and the Spirit in the New Testament,* ed. B. Lindars and S.S. Smalley (Cambridge, 1973).

34. *Theology of Liberation,* p. 166. A.G. Honig has correctly observed that it is of central import to the theology of liberation to overcome this dualism. Cf. A.G. Honig, *Jezus Christus de Bevrijder, de inhoud van de Missionaire verkondiging,* Kamper Cahiers no. 25 (Kampen, 1975), p. 12.

35. Gutiérrez, ibid.

36. Cf. H.N. Ridderbos, *Coming of the Kingdom,* pp. 106ff.

37. Cf. A. Plummer, *Luke,* in series *International Critical Commentary* (New York, 1922), p. 121.

38. Cf. M. Buthelezi, *Toward an African Theology,* Lectures given at the University of Heidelberg, 1972, p. 35. Cf. Ridderbos, *Coming of the Kingdom,* p. 185ff.

39. Plummer, *Luke.*

40. Stanton, *Jesus,* p. 77.

41. B. Maarsingh, *Leviticus,* in the series *De Prediking van het Oude Testament* (Nijkerk, 1974), pp. 228–41; also R. North, *Sociology of the Biblical Jubilee* (Rome, 1954); K. Barth, *K.D.* III/2 (Zürich, 1948), pp. 547–48.

42. Cf. Ridderbos, *Coming of the Kingdom,* p. 185; Metropolitan Paul Gregorios, "To Proclaim Liberation," in Richard D.N. Dickinson, *To Set at Liberty the Oppressed, Towards an Understanding of Christian Responsibilities for Development/Liberation,* W.C.C. (Lausanne, 1975) pp. 186–93.

43. *Coming of the Kingdom*, p. 185.

44. Ibid., p. 190.

45. Ibid.

46. Issued by the Theological Commission of the South African Council of Churches, June 1968.

47. Published in *Pro Veritate*, December 1975, under the title *A Namibian Letter: A Christian Message After Detention*.

48. See my "Swart en Blanke Vriende" in *Pro Veritate*, February 1974, in which I have tried to deal with the struggle of the so-called "Coloured" person with regard to this problem.

49. 1976 NCBC Statement on Black Theology.

50. While the Bible accepts self-love as a matter of course, self-denial is seen as the way toward self-fulfillment and self-determination. Cf. S.J. Ridderbos, "Het Voorwerp van de liefde," in *Bezinning*, no. 4, 1963, p. 193. Idem, *Ethiek van het Liefdesgebod* (Kampen, 1974).

51. Martin Luther King, Jr., J. Deotis Roberts, and others have pointed out that in most dictionaries the word "black" has a pejorative meaning. The Afrikaans/English *Groot Woordeboek* (1972 edition!) gives as the correct translation of "black person" the word "swart slang," "swartner." The translation of the English word "gentleman" is "witman" (white man). If we know that "gentle" is translated with "fatsoenlik" (decent), "beskaafd" (civilized), and "minsaam" (kind), the meaning and its implications are crystal clear. Black psychiatrists Cobbs and Grier discuss the destructive effects of self-hatred and self-alienation of black people. They speak of self-hatred, cultural paranoia, and cultural masochism as "simply adaptive devices developed in response to a peculiar environment. They represent normal devices for making it in America" (William H. Grier and Price M. Cobbs, *Black Rage* [New York, 1972], pp. 149–50).

52. Ernest Marshall Howse, *Saints in Politics* (London, 1973), p. 30.

53. Major Jones, *Black Awareness*, pp. 72–77.

54. Cf. François Houtart and André Rousseau, *The Church and Revolution*, English translation (Maryknoll, New York, 1971); also H. Gollwitzer, *Die Kapitalistische Revolution* (Münich, 1974); H. Achterhuis, *Uitgestelde Revolutie*.

55. G.J. Heering, *De Zondeval van het Christendom* (Utrecht, 1953). Although Prof. Heering deals with the surrender of Christendom to the forces of violence, his argumentation serves our case very well. Cf. also Gollwitzer, "Schwarze Theologie," in *Evangelische Theologie*, January 1974; J. van Raalte, *Secularisatie en zending in*

Suriname (Wageningen, 1973); F. Boerwinkel, *Einde of Nieuw Begin* (Bilthoven, 1974).

56. Gollwitzer, "Schwarze Theologie," pp. 45, 46.

57. Ibid., p. 48. See also *Kapitalistische Revolution*.

58. Ibid., p. 45. Translation ours.

59. Cited in ibid., p. 46.

60. Cited in Howse, *Saints*, p. 30.

61. Gayraud Wilmore, *Black Religion and Black Radicalism* (New York, 1972), pp. 34–36; Jones, *Black Awareness*, pp. 3, 4; also James Cone, *The Spirituals and the Blues* (New York, 1972), p. 23.

62. Jones, *Black Awareness*, pp. 38, 42.

63. Howse, *Saints*, p. 31.

64. P. Huet, *Het Lot der Zwarten in Transvaal, Mededeelingen omtrent Slavernij en wreedheden in de Z.A. Republiek* (Utrecht, 1869).

65. Ibid., pp. 29–30.

66. N. R. Rhoodie and H. Venter quote from *Die Kerbode* (September 22, 1948); "As a church we have always propagated the separation of the races. In this respect *Apartheid* may rightly be called a church policy" (*Apartheid*, p. 165). Cf. also G. Cronje, *Regverdige Rasse-apartheid* (Stellenbosch, 1947), pp. 33–34; also Allan Boesak, "Is Apartheid die Kerk se Skuld?" article in *Pro Veritate*, February 1973.

67. In G. Cronje, *Regverdige (Just Racial Apartheid)*. Also A.B. du Preez, *Eiesoortige Ontwikkeling tot Volksdiens* (Pretoria, 1958); also the different reports prepared by the Dutch Afrikaans churches for the Reformed Ecumenical Synod 1948–1972. An example from Groenewald: ". . . It can be stated with gratitude that the race policy of the Afrikaner testifies to the reverence [the Afrikaner] has for God and his Word" (p. 67).

68. In Cronje, *Regverdige*, p. 62.

69. *Ras, Volk, Nasie en Vookereverhoudinge in die Lig van die Skrif* (Cape Town/Pretoria, 1975), pp. 31, 72. My italics.

70. Cf. N.G.T.T., January 1973; also the report of the so-called Legrange Commission to the South African Government on the Christian Institute. A critique by Dr. Manas Buthelezi on the Report's treatment of Black Theology appeared in *Pro Veritate*, November 1975.

71. J. Mbiti, " 'Our Saviour' as an African Experience," in Smalley and Lindars, eds., *Christ and the Spirit*, pp. 400ff.

72. Ibid., p. 407.

73. Ibid., p. 410.

74. Wilmore, *Black Religion*, p. 5; also D.D.L. Makhatini, "Schwarze Theologie," in T. Sundermeier, ed., *Christus der Schwarze Befreier* (Erlangen, 1973), pp. 103ff; James Cone, *Spirituals*, p. 67.

75. Wilmore, *Black Religion,* p. 14.

76. Philip S. Foner, *Selections from the Writings of Frederick Douglass* (New York, 1964), p. 55.

77. B.M. Sundkler, *Bantu Prophets in South Africa* (London, 1961), p. 277.

78. Cf. ibid.; also Wilmore, *Black Religion,* pp. 52ff.

79. Cf. Wilmore, *Black Religion,* p. 40.

80. A. Kuyper, *De Crisis in Zuid-Afrika,* (Amsterdam, 1900), p. 21. Wilmore also testifies to this fact *(Black Religion,* chap. 5).

81. Cf. Wilmore, *Black Religion;* also Edward Roux, *Time Longer Than Rope, A History of the Black Man's Struggle for Freedom in South Africa* (Madison, Wisconsin, 1972); Monica Hunter, *Reaction to Conquest* (Cape Town, 1952).

82. Cf. Floyd B. Barbour, *The Black Power Revolt* (Boston, 1969), p. 41.

83. J.L. de Vries, "Sending en Kolonialisme in Suid-Wes Afrika," unpublished dissertation, Protestantse Theologische Fakulteit (Brussels: 1971), p. 183.

84. Ibid., pp. 183–84.

85. Ibid., p. 185.

86. D.D.L. Makhatini, "What is Black Theology?" Unpublished paper.

87. In an interview on African Theology and Black Theology in *AACC Bulletin,* July/August 1975.

88. James Cone, *God of the Oppressed* (New York, 1975), p. 11.

89. So correctly H.M. Kuitert, *De Spelers en het Spel* (Baarn, 1970), p. 52.

90. Vincent Harding, "Black Power and the American Christ," in Barbour, ed., *Black Power Revolt,* p. 86.

91. Cf. Albert Cleage, Jr., *The Black Messiah* (New York, 1968), passim.

92. 1976 NCBC Statement on Black Theology.

93. So the Dutch Reverend Coevorden with regard to the "Kaffirs" in South Africa, cited in Ben van Kaam, "Arbeid voor ongelovigen," in *Je Hoeft er niet geweest te zijn, Apartheid in de praktijk* (Baarn, 1973), p. 11.

94. Cf. the way G. ter Schegget writes about this in *Het Geheim van de Mens* (Baarn, 1973), pp. 33–38; also Karl Barth, *K.D.* 1V/2, 614ff.

Chapter Two

1. Cited in G.E. Langemeier, "Macht van Regeerders en Geregeerden," in *Macht, Voordrachten Gehouden in het kader van het*

Studium Generale van de Rijksuniversiteit Groningen (Haarlem, 1970), p. 27.

2. Cf. Langemeier, ibid.; cf. Bertrand Russell, *Power* (London, 1957); P. Thoenes, "Maatschappelijke Verdeling van de Macht," in *Macht*, p. 46.

3. Cf. Thoenes, "Maatschappelijke"; Charles Reich, *The Greening of America* (Penguin, 1971); Steven Lukes, *Power: A Radical View* (London, 1974). M. C. Rijk, *Structuur, Macht en Geweld* (Bloemendaal, 1972), pp. 80–99.

4. Johan Galtung, *The European Community: A Super Power in the Making* (Oslo-London, 1973), p. 33.

5. E.g., Martin Luther King, Jr., *Where Do We Go From Here: Chaos or Community?* (London, 1967), p. 37.

6. Thoenes, "Maatschappelijke," p. 47.

7. E. Ed Stern, *Macht door gehoorzaamheid, theologisch onderzoek naar de macht over mensen* (Baarn, 1973), p. 132.

8. Galtung, *European Community*, p. 33.

9. This fact was admirably demonstrated during the Russian occupation of Czechoslovakia, cf. Vladimir Horský, *Prag 1968, Systemveränderung und Systemverteidigung*. Studien zur Friedensforschung, 14 (Stuttgart/Munich, 1975), pp. 471ff. Horský writes: "Herrschaft hangt vom Gehorsam und von der Mitarbeit der Beherrschten ab; ist der Gehorsam aufgekündigt un Mitarbeit massenhaft und effektiv verweigert, kann sich keine Herrschaft à la longue behaupten" (p. 471).

10. Paul Tillich, *The Courage to Be* (New Haven, 1952).

11. Cf. A. Kruyswijk, *Geen Gesneden Beeld. . .* (Franeker, 1962), p. 194. Cf. also C. de Beus, *De Mens als het beeld Gods in het Oude en Nieuwe Testament* (The Hague: 1968).

12. Kruyswijk, ibid., p. 197.

13. J. Pedersen states: "The relation between the earth and its owner . . . is a covenant-relation, a psychic community, and the owner does not solely prevail in the relation. The earth has its nature, which makes itself felt, and demands respect. . . . The task of the peasant is to deal kindly with the earth, to uphold its blessing and then take what it yields of its own accord" (*Israel, Its Life and Culture* [Copenhagen-London, 1926], p. 479.

14. R. Guardini, *De Moderne mens en het probleem van de Macht* (Utrecht, 1959), p. 17.

15. Albert B. Cleage, Jr., *Black Christian Nationalism* (New York, 1972), p. 101.

16. Cf. Allan Boesak, *Coming in Out of the Wilderness: A Comparative*

Interpretation of the Ethics of Martin Luther King and Malcolm X, Kamper Cahier No. 28 (Kampen, 1976).

17. Stern, *Macht door gehoorzaamheid,* pp. 7–20, especially pp. 17ff.

18. A.J. Rasker, "Macht, Ethische aspecten," in *Macht, Voordrachten,* pp. 20–21.

19. Stern, *Macht door gehoorzaamheid,* p. 19.

20. May, *Power and Innocence,* p. 102.

21. S. Carmichael and V. Hamilton, *Black Power: The Politics of Liberation in America* (New York, 1967).

22. Ibid., p. 8.

23. Ibid., p. 3.

24. Apart from the institutional violence inherent to South African society, this escalation is evident in the staggering amount budgeted for defense in 1975—R948 million. Cf. *The Star,* March 27, 1975. The *Star* editorial tacitly commented: "However, within this framework, the Budget remains a painful reminder of the distortions, the stresses and the potential dangers inherent in South African society." Indeed.

25. Peter Randall on education in *Pro Veritate,* August 1973.

26. King voiced his critique in *Chaos or Community,* chap. 2.

27. Ibid., p. 33.

28. Ibid., p. 37.

29. Ibid.

30. Ibid.

31. Ibid., p. 38.

32. Ibid.

33. Ibid., pp. 40–41.

34. Ibid., p. 48.

35. Ibid., p. 44.

36. Ibid., p. 52.

37. Ibid., p. 62.

38. Ibid., p. 64.

39. Joseph R. Washington, *Black and White Power Subreption* (Boston, 1969).

40. Ibid., p. 199.

41. Ibid.

42. Ibid.

43. Ibid., p. 200.

44. Ibid., p. 203.

45. Ibid., p. 202.

46. Ibid.

47. Cited in Barbour, *Black Power Revolt,* p. 23.

48. Ibid., pp. 34–41.

49. Ibid., p. 43.

50. Cf. Sundkler, *Bantu Prophets*, p. 179.

51. Roux, *Time Longer than Rope*, p. 18.

52. *Pro Veritate*, October 1973.

53. *Chaos or Community*, pp. 40–41.

54. Carmichael and Hamilton, *Black Power*, p. 47.

55. Ibid., p. 50.

56. James Baldwin, *The Fire Next Time* (New York, 1963), p. 34.

57. Cf. C. Eric Lincoln, *The Black Muslims in America* (Boston, 1961), p. 87.

58. Vincent Harding, "The Religion of Black Power," in *The Religious Situation* (Boston, 1968), pp. 21–22.

59. Cf. Boesak, *Coming in Out of the Wilderness*, especially chap. 5.

60. Cf. Boesak, ibid.; David Halberstam, "When Civil Rights and Peace Join Forces," in C. Eric Lincoln, ed., *Martin Luther King, Jr.: A Profile* (New York, 1970).

61. *Chaos or Community*, p. 65.

62. Ibid., p. 66.

63. Dietrich Bonhoeffer, *Ethik*, 7th ed. (Munich, 1966), pp. 233–34.

64. I am thankful to Prof. Wilmore, who opened this perspective to me in a personal communication.

Chapter Three

1. I find it difficult to assess what Cone really says on this point. Black Power is indeed not the gospel, but it is "Christ's central message to 20th century America," it is Christianity, etc. Likewise, Cone says that "the black revolution is the work of Christ" without further qualification. However one looks at it, the uneasy feeling persists that in Cone's first work he is on the very edge of identifying the gospel with the political program of Black Power.

2. James Cone, *Black Theology*, pp. 6, 22.

3. Ibid., p. 8.

4. Ibid., p. 1.

5. Ibid., p. 38.

6. Ibid., p. 37.

7. Ibid., p. 38.

8. Ibid., p. 39.

9. Ibid.

10. Ibid., p. 58.

11. Ibid.

12. Ibid., p. 61.

13. Ibid., p. 60.

14. Ibid., pp. 1, 41. Our emphasis.

15. Ibid., p. 62.

16. Ibid., p. 61.

17. Cf. chap. 2, note 39.

18. *Black and White Power Subreption*, p. 190, also pp. 117–23.

19. Ibid., p. 196.

20. Ibid., p. 121.

21. Ibid., p. 125.

22. Ibid., p. 129.

23. Ibid., p. 128.

24. Ibid., p. 179.

25. Cf. the contributions of Pityana, Steve Biko, and M. Mothlabi in Basil Moore, *Schwarze Theologie in Sudafrika, Dokumente einer Bewegung* (Göttingen, 1973).

26. Moore, ibid.

27. Mothlabi, in ibid.

28. Simon Maimela, "Die Relevanz Schwarzer Theologie," in Sundermeier, *Christus*, pp. 109–21.

29. Ibid., p. 109.

30. Ibid.

31. Ibid., pp. 115–16. Our emphasis.

32. Cleage, *Black Messiah*, p. 54.

33. *Black Christian Nationalism*, p. xix.

34. Vincent Harding, "The Religion of Black Power," in *The Religious Situation* (Boston, 1968).

35. J. Deotis Roberts, *Liberation and Reconciliation: A Black Theology* (Philadelphia, 1970), p. 19.

36. Ibid., p. 55.

37. Ibid., p. 86.

38. Ibid., p. 87.

39. Ibid., p. 98.

40. Ibid., p. 193.

41. Roberts, *A Black Political Theology* (Philadelphia, 1974), p. 144.

42. Buthelezi, "Black Theology and African Theology," in Moore, *Schwarze Theologie*.

43. Ibid.

44. Ernest Baartman, "Was Bedeuter die Entwicklung des Schwarzes Bewusstseins für die Kirche?" in Sundermeier, *Christus*, pp. 85–93.

45. "Ich glaube, dass zu Black Power Gewaltanwendung gehört" (ibid., p. 88).

46. Ibid.

47. Ibid.

48. Cf. Sundermeier, *Christus,* Introduction; D. Bosch, "Stromingen in de Zuid Afrikaanse Zwarte Theologie," in *Evangelie in Afrikaans Gewaad* (Kampen, 1974); idem, "Navolging van Christus in Suid- en Suid-Wes Afrika Vandag," paper published by the Christian Academy of South Africa.

49. *Lectures,* p. 15.

50. Ibid., p. 16.

51. Ibid.

52. Ibid.

53. In *Pro Veritate,* April 1973.

54. K.-H. DeJung has correctly emphasized the important place this notion occupies in the theology of Thomas. Cf. K.-H. DeJung, *Die Oekumenische Bewegung im Entwicklungskonflikt 1910–1969,* Studien zur Friedensforschung, no. 11 (Stuttgart/Munich, 1973).

55. H.H. Wolf's reaction was published in *The Ecumenical Review,* January 1966; the W.C.C. picked up the theme again in its studies on God in nature and history; in Holland, e.g., A.G. Honig continued the discussion in subsequent publications, and Lehmann's *Ethics in a Christian Context* (New York, 1963) also deals with this theme.

56. *Ecumenical Review,* January 1966, p. 23.

57. Ibid., p. 24.

58. Ibid.

59. Ibid.

60. Dejung, *Oekumenische Bewegung,* p. 443.

61. Ibid.

62. M.M. Thomas, "Issues Concerning the Life and Work of the Church in a Revolutionary World," in A.H. van den Heuvel, ed., *Unity of Mankind,* W.C.C. (Geneva, 1969), pp. 89–98.

63. Ibid.

64. In *Ecumenical Review,* January 1966.

65. Ibid., p. 19.

66. Ibid., p. 12.

67. Ibid.

68. Ibid., p. 13.

69. Ibid.

70. A.G. Honig, *Meru en Golgotha* (Franeker, 1969).

71. Ibid., p. 309.

72. Ibid., p. 310, with reference to the Barmen Declaration.

73. Ibid., p. 313.

74. Ibid., p. 315.

75. Ibid., p. 317.

76. *Ecumenical Review*, January 1966, p. 24.

77. *Meru en Golgotha* p. 307: "Vervolgens omdat het een oneindig grotere verzoeking is voor kerken in Afrika en Azië, om in de huidige revolutie Christus ook aan het werk te zien. . . . De Nederlandse christenen kunnen wat in Nederland gebeurt—zeer terecht [*sic!*]— niet los zien van wat Christus via het evangelie doet."

78. *Ecumenical Review*, p. 18.

79. Ibid., p. 25.

80. Ibid., p. 22. Our emphasis.

81. Cf. Thomas, "Issues," p. 92.

82. Honig, *Meru en Golgotha*, p. 317.

83. A.G. Honig, *De Kosmische betekenis van Christus*, Kamper Cahier no. 7 (Kampen, 1968), p. 18. Our emphasis.

84. Ibid., p. 20.

85. Ibid.

86. Lehmann, *Ethics*, p. 75.

87. Cf. ibid., p. 78.

88. Ibid., p. 80. Cf. Rom. 7:15.

89. Ibid., p. 117.

90. Cf. DeJung, *Oekumenische Bewegung*, p. 447.

91. Rasker, "Macht, Ethische aspecten," p. 23.

92. Ibid.

93. Cf. H. Wiersinga, *Verzoening als Verandering* (Baarn, 1973), p. 13.

94. Ibid., p. 105.

95. May, *Power and Innocence*, p. 253.

96. M.H. Bolkenstein, *De Brieven van Petrus en Judas*, in the series *De Prediking van het Nieuwe Testament* (Nijkerk, 1963), p. 116.

97. Ibid., p. 117.

98. Cf. ibid.; also H.N. Ridderbos, *Paulus, Ontwerp van Zijn Theologie* (Kampen, 1966), pp. 352ff. This is with regard to the position of Paul on this subject.

99. Bolkenstein, *Brieven*, p. 117.

100. C. Klapwijk, *Vreugde en lijden, sociaal masochistische trekken in het christendom* (Kampen, 1974), p. 73. For a thorough discussion of suffering as a reality in Christian life see Klapwijk, *Sociaal masochisme en christelijk ethos*, een confrontatie met Th. Reiks interpretatie van het christendom (Kampen, 1973).

101. M. Buthelezi, "The Significance of the Christian Institute for Black South Africa," in *L. W. F. Information*, June 1975. Cf. also Klapwijk, *Sociaal masochisme*, pp. 143ff, 163ff.

102. Martin Luther King, Jr., *Stride Toward Freedom, The Montgomery Story* (New York, 1964), p. 193.

103. Cone, *Black Theology and Black Power,* p. 52.

104. Paul Tillich, *Love, Power and Justice,* 2nd ed. (New York, 1972), p. 49.

105. Cone, *God of the Oppressed,* pp. 84–85.

106. Cf. Maimela, "Relevanz," p. 117; Cleage, *Black Messiah,* passim.

107. G.T. Rothuizen, *Wat is Ethiek?* (Kampen, 1973), p. 35.

108. Ibid., p. 124.

Chapter Four

1. Cf. A.S. Geyser, "Ideologie," in *Pro Veritate,* November 1967; J. Sperna Weiland, "Theologie en Ideologie," in *Rondom het Woord,* November 1973; Karl Mannheim, *Ideology and Utopia,* 9th ed. (London, 1972); and also André Dumas, "The Ideological Factor in the West," in M. de Vries, ed., *Man in Community,* W.C.C. (London-New York, 1966); J. Verkuyl, *Inleiding in de Nieuwere Zendingswetenschap* (Kampen, 1975), chap. 14.

2. Cf. Dumas, ibid., p. 63.

3. It is noteworthy that Sir Francis Bacon indicated the distinction between the "idola tribus," illusions inherent in the human mind, the "idola specus," errors peculiar to particular individuals, the "idola fori," false concepts derived from current language, and the "idola theatri," the speculations of philosophers. Thus, long before Marx, Bacon thought of "ideologies," which for him denoted the speculative idolatry that impedes true scientific knowledge. Cf. Dumas, ibid.; Mannheim, *Ideology and Utopia,* p. 55.

4. Cf. Karl Marx, "Die Deutsche Ideologie," *Marx/Engels Gesammtausgabe* III (Berlin, 1964).

5. Cf. Dumas, "Ideological Factor," p. 65. Dumas contends that Marx actually proposes two different concepts of ideology. First, ideology as described. Secondly, Marxism presents itself as the only true ideology (p. 67).

6. *Ideology and Utopia,* pp. 173–75.

7. Ibid., p. 173.

8. Risto Lehtonen, Introduction, in *Ideologies, Student World,* nos. 3 and 4 (Geneva, 1969).

9. Ibid.

10. Ibid.

11. Ibid.

12. Albert Stüttgen, *Kriterien einer Ideologiekritik* (Mainz, 1972), pp. 37–66.

13. Ibid., p. 68.

14. Cf. J. Sperna Weiland, "Theologie en Ideologie."

15. J. Verkuyl, *In leiding*, pp. 94–95; idem, *Breek de Muren af! Over gerechtigheid in rassenverhoudingen* (Baarn, 1969), pp. 96–102. Dumas, "Ideological Factor," p. 62.

16. Dumas, ibid., p. 62.

17. C.J. Labuschagne, *Schriftprofetie en Volksideologie* (Nijerk, 1968).

18. Ibid., p. 12.

19. Cf. J.T. Bakker in "Gereformeerd Weekblad," October 12, 1973. He compares this to a recent article of Dr. J.D. Vorster and clearly shows how the gospel is still used in this ideological way.

20. J. Sperna Weiland, "Theologie en Ideologie." He confines himself to ideologies which are "not aware of their ideological character."

21. The "theology of revolution" debate is a clear illustration of this fact. H.M. Kuitert has conclusively shown that the question: "Was Jesus a revolutionary?" is never asked in a disinterested way. There is always a host of factors which bias the questioner. Kuitert therefore advises not to pretend that these questions could be asked disinterestedly, but, rather, to ask them with the right interests in mind: those of the other. Cf. H.M. Kuitert: *Om em Om* (Kampen, 1972), pp. 137–57. On the theology of revolution, cf. *Diskussion zur Theologie der Revolution*, ed. E. Feil and R. Weth; M. Hengel, *War Jesus Revolutionar?* (Stuttgart, 1970); S.G. Brandon, *Jesus and the Zealots* (London, 1967); O. Cullmann, *Jesus und die Revolutionaren Seiner Zeit* (Tübingen, 1970).

22. *God of the Oppressed*, p. 97.

23. J. Sperna Weiland, "Theologie en Ideologie."

24. J.B. Metz, *Zur Theologie der Welt* (Munich, 1968), pp. 99–107. Also H.M. Kuitert, *De Realiteit van het Geloof* (Kampen, 1966), pp. 91ff.

25. Metz, ibid.

26. Rubem Alves, *A Theology of Human Hope* (New York, 1975), pp. 34–43.

27. Ibid., p. 43.

28. "Theologie en Ideologie."

29. *Ras, Volk, Nasie en Volkereverhoudinge*. Cf. chap. 1, note 69.

30. Cf. passages on Christian love, social justice, and human rights, and sentences like: "The Christian must have the freedom to exercise political thought and action in a responsible way in the light of the Word of God" (p. 72); and "When rights and privileges are rightfully claimed, they should not be withheld [from people]" (p. 72; cf. further pp. 33–34, 65–67).

31. Ibid., pp. 94–101.

32. Cf. ibid., pp. 84ff. This present attitude of the white Dutch Reformed church is strongly reminiscent of the attitude of the church in 1857, when it first decided to have segregated services (and later segregated churches) "because of the weakness of some." With regard to the 1857 decision, D.P. Botha writes: "It is clear that from then on, Scripture would not be the absolute norm for the church as was the case during the previous century" (D.P. Botha, *Die Opkoms van ons Derdestand* [Cape Town, 1960], p. 73).

33. Juan Antonio Franco Medina, "The Showcase for Democracy Shatters: Puerto Rico, 1969," in *Student World*, nos. 3 and 4 (Geneva, 1969).

34. Francis Wilson, *Migrant Labour in South Africa* (Johannesburg, 1972), especially chaps. 8, 9, and 10.

35. Ibid., p. 189.

36. *Landman Report*, p. 75.

37. Ibid., p. 65.

38. Labuschagne's Dutch formulation is even most cogent: "Klopt de realiteit niet met het dogma, des te erger voor de realiteit!" (*Schriftprofetie*, p. 15).

39. A dictum of G.F. Froneman, Administrator of the Orange Free State, according to the *Rand Daily Mail* and *Pro Veritate*, August 1972.

40. *Pro Veritate*, August 1972.

41. Labuschagne, *Schriftprofetie*, p. 12.

42. "Christian Nationalism," in T. Sundermeier, ed., *The Church and Nationalism* (Johannesburg, 1975).

43. Ibid.

44. Ibid.

45. Ibid.

46. Ibid.

47. Cited by Cedric Mason, "Deliverance From Group Justification," in *Pro Veritate*, November 1972.

48. "Christian Nationalism."

49. A.M. Hugo, "Christelik-Nasionaal in Suid Afrika Vandage," in *Pro Veritate*, May 1968.

50. Ibid.

51. Ibid.

52. Ibid.

53. Ibid.

54. Ibid.

55. Ibid.

56. Ibid.

57. Ibid.

58. Mannheim, *Ideology and Utopia*, pp. 86–87. Cf. P. Berger and R. Neuhaus, *Movement and Revolution* (New York, 1970), pp. 14ff.

59. Cf. Cleage, *The Black Messiah; Black Christian Nationalism*.

60. *Black Christian Nationalism*, p. xv.

61. Ibid., p. 174.

62. Ibid., p. xxvi.

63. Ibid., p. 106.

64. Ibid., pp. 174–76.

65. *Black Messiah*, pp. 39–42.

66. *Black Messiah*, pp. 90, 91.

67. *Black Christian Nationalism*, p. 40.

68. Ibid.

69. *Black Messiah*, pp. 37, 87.

70. Ibid., p. 215.

71. *Black Christian Nationalism*, p. 40.

72. *Black Messiah*, p. 163.

73. *Black Messiah*, p. 97; also: *Black Christian Nationalism*, pp.150ff.

74. Cf. J. Deotis Roberts, *Liberation and Reconciliation*, pp.55ff.

75. Ibid., p. 137.

76. Cf. Roelf Meyer and Beyers Naudé, "Geloftedag: Christusfees of Baälfees, 'n Ope Vraag aan Suid Afrika oor Geloftedag," supplement to *Pro Veritate*, December 1971.

77. Gollwitzer, "Schwarze Theologie," in *Evangelische Theologie*, January 1973.

78. Ibid.

79. *Schriftprofetie*, p. 15.

Chapter Five

1. Manas Buthelezi, "African Theology or Black Theology," in Moore, *Schwarze Theologie*.

2. *A Black Theology of Liberation*, p. 23.

3. Ibid., p. 12.

4. *Black Theology and Black Power*, pp. 6, 22. In *Liberation*, Cone phrases it thus: "The role of Black Theology is to tell black people to focus on their own self-determination as a community by preparing to do anything which the community believes to be necessary for its existence" (p. 41).

5. *Liberation*, p. 129.

6. *Black Theology and Black Power*, p. 52.

7. Ibid., p. 53.

8. *Liberation*, p. 137.

9. Ibid., pp. 131–32.

10. Ibid., p. 132.

11. Ibid., p. 138.

12. *Black Theology and Black Power*, p. 143.

13. Ibid.

14. Ibid., p. 146.

15. Cone, "Black Theology and Reconciliation," in *Christianity and Crisis*, January 22, 1973.

16. Ibid.

17. Washington, *Black and White Power Subreption*, p. 120.

18. Ibid., p. 118.

19. Ibid., p. 179.

20. Ibid., p. 186.

21. Ibid., p. 187.

22. Preston Williams, "James Cone and the Problem of a Black Ethic," in *Harvard Theological Review* 65, 1972, pp. 483–94.

23. Ibid., p. 485.

24. Ibid., p. 487.

25. Ibid., p. 488.

26. Ibid.

27. Ibid., p. 489.

28. Martin Luther King, Jr., *The Trumpet of Conscience* (London, 1968), p. 57.

29. Cf. chap. 3, note 35.

30. Ibid., p. 13.

31. Ibid., p. 182.

32. Ibid., p. 27.

33. Ibid., p. 24.

34. Ibid., p. 19.

35. Ibid., p. 24.

36. Ibid., p. 191.

37. Ibid., p. 193.

38. Ibid., p. 101.

39. Ibid., p. 120.

40. Ibid., p. 159.

41. Ibid., p. 196.

42. Ibid., p. 187.

43. Ibid., p. 184.

44. Ibid.

45. Ibid., p. 190.

46. Ibid.

47. Ibid.

48. Ibid., p. 194.

49. Ibid.

50. Ibid., p. 198.

51. Major J. Jones, *Awareness* (cf. Introduction, note 13); idem, *Christian Ethics for Black Theology* (Nashville, 1974).

52. *Awareness*, p. 70.

53. Small, "Schwarzsein gegen den Nihilismus," in Moore, *Schwarze Theologie*.

54. *Awareness*, pp. 74–75, 77–84.

55. Ibid., p. 80.

56. Ibid., p. 82.

57. *Christian Ethics*, p. 147.

58. *Awareness*, p. 83.

59. *Christian Ethics*, p. 71.

60. *Awareness*, p. 95.

61. *Christian Ethics*, p. 150.

62. Ibid., p. 199.

63. Small, "Schwarzsein."

64. Ibid.

65. Ibid.

66. Cf. Pityana, Biko, and Mothlabi, in Moore, *Schwarze Theologie*.

67. Makhatini, "Black Theology—What Is It?" Paper.

68. Mothlabi, "Schwarze Theologie aus personlicher Sicht," in Moore, *Schwarze Theologie*.

69. A. Zulu, "Whither Black Theology?" in *Pro Veritate*, March 1973.

70. Ibid.

71. It is very interesting to note that D. Bosch, while making use of his criticism by Zulu, quotes him without completing Zulu's sentence: ". . . after gaining liberation." Anyway Zulu adds, ". . . the experience which has given birth to Black Theology is unknown to white theologians . . . " (ibid.) Cf. D. Bosch, *Evangelie in Afrikaans Gewaad*, pp. 113ff. I am grateful to Dr. K.-H. DeJung who pointed this out to me.

72. Biko, in Moore, *Schwarze Theologie*.

73. Ibid.

74. C. Eric Lincoln, "Antwort aus Schwarzer Perspektive," in *Evangelische Theologie*, January 1974.

75. Cf. H.J. Heering, *Ethiek der Voorlopigheid*, 2nd ed. (Nijkerk, 1972), p. 48.

76. Rothuizen, *Wat is Ethiek?* pp. 26–29.

77. "Maar pas wanneer ethiek, behalve sociaal, ook politiek is, is ze 'rond,' is ze helemaal ethiek" (p. 30). Indeed!

78. J.M. Lochman, "The Just Revolution," in *Christianity & Crisis,* July 10, 1972.

79. In an unpublished speech to SCLC leadership, February 23, 1968.

80. A.J. Rasker, *Theologie und Revolution,* Evangelische Zeitstimmen (Hamburg, 1969), p. 11.

81. Cf. Martin Luther King's conception of agape in *Stride Toward Freedom;* also *Strength to Love* (London, 1970). Cf. also James Cone, *Black Theology and Black Power,* pp. 47ff.

82. Ridderbos, *Coming of the Kingdom,* p. 190. Emphasis added.

83. Washington, *Black and White Power Subreption,* p. 200.

84. Ibid., p. 118.

85. Apart from the utterances in several works on Black Theology, this is amply illustrated in Cone's discussion with Latin American theologians. Cf. the special issue of *Risk,* "Incommunication," WCC, Geneva, vol. 9., no. 2, 1973, pp. 21, 62.

86. Cf. Boesak, *Coming in out of the Wilderness.*

87. *Liberation,* p. 37.

88. Ibid., p. 41.

89. *Evangelische Theologie,* January 1974.

90. In *Evangelische Theologie,* January 1974.

91. Ibid.

92. *Evangelische Theologie.*

93. Alves, "Christian Realism, Ideology of the Establisment," in *Christianity & Crisis,* September 17, 1973.

SELECTED BIBLIOGRAPHY

BLACK THEOLOGY AND BLACK POWER

Achterhuis, Hans. *De uitgestelde revolutie, over ontwikkeling en apartheid*. Baarn, 1973.

Adam, Herbert. "The Rise of Black Consciousness in South Africa." In *Race*, Journal of the Institute of Race Relations (London), vol. 15, no. 2 (1973).

Allen, Richard. *The Life Experiences and Gospel Labors of the Rt. Rev. Richard Allen*. New York-Nashville, 1960.

Baartman, Ernest. "The Black and the Church." In *Pro Veritate* (Johannesburg), April 1973.

Barbour, Floyd. *The Black Power Revolt*. Boston, 1969.

Boesak, Allan. *Coming in out of the Wilderness. A Comparative Interpretation of the Ethics of Martin Luther King, Jr., and Malcolm X*. Kamper Cahier No. 28. Kampen, 1976.

Boesak, Allan, ed. *Om her zwart te zeggen*. Kampen, 1976.

Boesak, Allan. "Zwarte Theologie." In *Voorlopig* (Delft-Kampen), October 1973; also in *Pro Veritate*, February 1974.

Bosch, D. *Het Evangelie in Afrikaans gewaad*. Kampen, 1973.

Bosch, D. "Navolging van Jezus Christus in Suid-en Suid-Wes Afrika Vandag." In stenciled booklet, Christian Academy of South Africa. Johannesburg, 1974.

Buthelezi, Manas. "Black Theology and the Le Grange-Schlebusch Commission." In *Pro Veritate*, October 1975.

Buthelezi, Manas. "The Christian Challenge of Black Theology." Unpublished paper.

Buthelezi, Manas. "The Meaning of the Christian Institute for Black South Africa." In *L.W.F. Information*, June 1975.

Buthelezi, Manas. "The Relevance of Black Theology." In stenciled booklet, Christian Academy of South Africa. Johannesburg, 1974.

Buthelezi, Manas. "Towards an African Theology." Lectures given at the University of Heidelberg, Germany, 1972.

Carmichael, S., and Hamilton, V. *Black Power: The Politics of Liberation in America*. New York, 1967.

Cleage, Albert B., Jr. *The Black Messiah*. New York, 1968.

Cleage, Albert B., Jr. *Black Christian Nationalism*. New York, 1972.

Cone, James H. "Black Power, Black Theology and the Study of Christian Ethics." Paper. 1970.

Cone, James H. *Black Theology and Black Power*. New York, 1969.

Cone, James H. "Black Theology and Reconciliation." In *Christianity & Crisis*, January 22, 1973.

Cone, James H. *A Black Theology of Liberation*. New York, 1972.

Cone, James H. *God of the Oppressed*. New York, 1975.

Cone, James H. "The Social Context of Theology: Freedom, History and Hope." In *Risk*, vol.9, no. 2, 1973.

Cone, James H. *The Spirituals and the Blues*. New York, 1972.

Cone, James H., and Wilmore, G. "Black Theology and African Theology." In *Pro Veritate*, January-February 1972.

Eichelberger, W.L. "Reflections on the Person and Personality of the Black Messiah." In *The Black Church*, vol. 2, no. 1 (Boston, 1973).

Essien-Udom, E.U. *Black Nationalism, A Search for an Identity in America*. New York, 1964.

Hanson, Geddes. "Black Theology and Protestant Thought." In *Social Progress*, September-October, 1969.

Harding, Vincent. "The Religion of Black Power." In *The Religious Situation*. Boston, 1968.

Hoyt, Robert S. "A Theology of Power." Unpublished paper.

Jones, Lawrence. "They Sought a City: The Black Church and Churchmen in the Nineteenth Century." In *Union Seminary Quarterly Review*, Spring 1971.

Jones, Major J. *Black Awareness: A Theology of Hope*. Nashville-New York, 1970.

Jones, Major J. *Christian Ethics for Black Theology*. Nashville-New York, 1974.

Jones, Miles J. "Toward a Theology of the Black Experience." In *Christian Century*, September 16, 1970.

Jones, William R. *Is God a White Racist? A Preamble to Black Theology*. Garden City, New York, 1973.

Kelsey, George. *Racism and the Christian Understanding of Man*. New York, 1965.

King, Martin Luther, Jr. *Strength to Love*. London, 1970.

King, Martin Luther, Jr. *Stride Toward Freedom: The Montgomery Story*. New York, 1964.

King, Martin Luther, Jr. "The Time Is Winding Up." In *Quarterly Magazine of the Fellowship of Reconciliation*, June 1968.

King, Martin Luther, Jr. *The Trumpet of Conscience*. London, 1968.

King, Martin Luther, Jr. *Where Do We Go From Here? Chaos or Community?* London, 1968.

King, Martin Luther, Jr. *Why We Can't Wait*. New York, 1968.

Lincoln, C. Eric. *The Black Muslims in America*. Boston, 1961.

Lincoln, C. Eric, ed. *Is Anybody Listening to Black America?* New York, 1968.

Lincoln, C. Eric, ed. *Martin Luther King, Jr.: A Profile*. New York, 1970.

Lomax, Louis. *The Negro Revolt*. New York, 1966.

Lomax, Louis. *To Kill a Black Man*. Los Angeles, 1968.

Lomax, Louis. *When the Word is Given*. New York, 1963.

Mays, Benjamin. *The Negro's God as Reflected in His Literature*. New York, 1973.

Mbiti, John. *African Religions and Philosophies*. Garden City, New York, 1970.

McClain, William. "The Genius of the Black Church." In *Christianity & Crisis*, November 1970.

Moore, Basil, ed. *Schwarze Theologie, Dokumente Einer Bewegung*. Gottingen, 1973. English edition: *Black Theology, the South African Voice*. London, 1973. Dutch edition: *Zwarte Theologie in Zuid-Afrika*. Baarn, 1974.

Roberts, J. Deotis. *A Black Political Theology*. Philadelphia, 1974.

Roberts, J. Deotis. "Black Theology and the Theological Revolution." In *Journal of Religious Thought*, Spring 1971.

Roberts, J. Deotis. *Liberation and Reconciliation: A Black Theology*. Philadelphia, 1970.

Skinner, Tom. *How Black is the Gospel?* Philadelphia, 1970.

Sundermeier, T., ed. *Christus, der schwarze Befreier*. Erlangen, 1973.

Thurman, Howard. *Jesus and the Disinherited*. Nashville-New York, 1970.

Traynham, Warner. *Christian Faith in Black and White, A Primer in Theology from the Black Perspective*. Wakefield, 1973.

Walshe, Peter. *Black Nationalism in South Africa*. Johannesburg, 1974.

Washington, Joseph R. *Black and White Power Subreption*. Boston, 1969.

Washington, Joseph R. *Black Religion*. Boston, 1964.

Washington, Joseph R. *The Politics of God*. Boston, 1967.

Williams, Preston. "James Cone and the Problem of a Black Ethic." In *Harvard Theological Review*, no. 65, 1972.

Wilmore, Gayraud S. *Black Religion and Black Radicalism.* New York, 1972.

Wilmore, Gayraud S. "Black Theology, Its Significance for Christian Mission Today." In *International Review of Mission,* vol. 63, April 1974.

Zulu, A. "Whither Black Theology?" In *Pro Veritate,* March 1973.

REPORTS, SPECIAL ISSUES ETC.

SPROCAS Reports (published jointly by the Christian Institute of Southern Africa and the South African Council of Churches, Johannesburg)

Education Beyond Apartheid, education commission report, 1971.
Towards Social Change, social commission report, 1972.
Power, Privilege and Poverty, economics commission report, 1972.
Law, Justice and Society, legal commission report, 1972.
Apartheid and the Church, church commission report, 1972.

Dutch Reformed Church Reports

A Plea for Understanding, A Reply to the Reformed Church in America. Ed. W.A. Landman (at the request of the Moderamen of the Dutch Reformed Church in South Africa (white). Cape Town, 1968.

Ras, Volk en Nasie en Volkereverhoudinge in die lig van die Skrif (Landman Report), commissioned for the General Synod of the Dutch Reformed Church (white). Cape Town-Pretoria, 1975.

W.C.C. Studies

The New Delhi Report, W.C.C. New York, 1962.
World Conference on Church and Society, Official Report, W.C.C. Geneva, 1967.
Uppsala Speaks, W.C.C. Fourth Assembly Section Reports. Geneva, 1969.
Unity of Mankind. Ed. A.H. van den Heuvel. Fourth Assembly Speeches. Geneva, 1969.
Conflict, Violence and Peace. Ed. Anwar Barkat. Geneva, 1970.
The Humanum Studies, 1969–1975. Geneva, 1975.

To Break the Chains of Oppression. CCPD Development Studies, no. 4. Geneva-Lausanne, 1975.

Violence, Non-violence and the Struggle for Social Justice. Geneva, 1973.

Ministry in Context. Theological Education Fund Study. London, 1970.

Learning in Context. T.E.F. Study. London, 1973.

Viability in Context. Ed. Herbert M. Zorn. T.E.F. Study. London, 1975.

Other Reports

The Struggle Continues. Official Report of the 3rd Assembly of the All Africa Conference of Churches. Lusaka, Nairobi, 1975.

Non-violent Action. A Report commissioned for the Reformed Church. London, 1973.

Theology in Action. Workshop Report. East Asian Christian Conference. Tokyo-Perth, 1973.

Ideologies, Options for Today. Special issue, *Student World*, nos. 34. Geneva, 1969.

Schwarze Theologie. Special issue, *Evangelische Theologie*, January 1974.

Swart Teologie. Special issue, *Nederduits Gereformeerde Teologiese Tydskrif.* January 1973.

Bevrijding. Special issue, in the series *Rondom het Woord.* Kampen, November 1974.

The Black Church. Special issue, *Christianity & Crisis*, November 2, 1970.

OTHER

Allmen, D. von D. "The Birth of Theology." In *International Review of Mission*, vol. 64, January 1975.

Alves, Rubem. "Christian Realism: Ideology of the Establishment." In *Christianity & Crisis*, September 17, 1973.

Alves, Rubem. *A Theology of Human Hope.* New York, 1975.

Assmann, Hugo. *Theology for a Nomad Church.* Maryknoll, New York, 1976.

Baird, J. Arthur. *The Justice of God in the Teaching of Jesus.* London, 1963.

Bakker, J.T. *Ook al ben je er geweest. . . .* Report of a trip to South Africa. In *Gereformeerd Weekblad*, October 26, November 1, and November 8, 1974.

178   *Selected Bibliography*

Baldwin, James. *The Fire Next Time.* New York, 1963.
Baldwin, James. *No Name in the Street.* London, 1973.
Baldwin, James. *Nobody Knows My Name.* London, 1973.
Baldwin, James. *Notes of a Native Son.* London, 1970.
Barclay, William. *Jesus as They Saw Him.* London, 1963.
Barth, K. *Kirchliche Dogmatik.* IV/2. Zurich, 1955.
Becken, H.-J., ed. *Relevant Theology for Africa.* Durban, 1973.
Bennett, J.C., ed. *Christian Social Ethics in a Changing World: An Ecumenical Inquiry.* London-New York, 1966.
Berkhof, H. *Christus de zin der geschiedenis.* Nijkerk: 1966.
Berger, Peter, and Neuhaus, Richard. *Movement and Revolution: On American Radicalism.* New York, 1970.
Biersteker, H., ed. *Macht over macht, veranderende opvattingen over gezag en macht.* Bilthoven, 1975.
duBois, W.E.B. *The Souls of Black Folk.* New York, 1961.
Bonhoeffer, D. *Ethik.* Munich, 1966.
Botha, D.P. *Die opkoms van ons derdestand.* Cape Town, 1960.
Brookes, Edgar. *Apartheid, A Documentary Study of Modern South Africa.* London, 1969.
Brown, Robert McAfee. *Religion and Violence.* Philadelphia, 1973.
Buber, M. *Schriften zur Bibel.* Werke II. Munich, 1964.
Camara, Helder. *Church and Colonialism.* London, 1969.
Conzelmann, H. *Die Mitte der Zeit. Studien zur Theologie des Lukas.* Tübingen, 1962.
Cullmann, O. *Jesus und die Revolutionären seiner Zeit.* Tübingen, 1970.
Daube, D. *The Exodus Pattern in the Bible.* London, 1963.
Degenhardt, H.-J. *Lukas, Evangelist der Armen.* Stuttgart, 1965.
DeJung, K.-H. *Die Oekumenische Bewegung im Entwicklungskonflikt, 1910–1968.* Studien zur Friedensforschung, Band 11. Stuttgart-Munich, 1973.
Dickinson, Richard. *To Set at Liberty the Oppressed. Towards an Understanding of Christian Responsibility for Development/Liberation.* CCPD, WCC. Geneva-Lausanne, 1975.
Ecumenical Review. Vol. 18, no. 1, January 1966.
Ecumenical Review. Vol. 24, no. 3, July 1972.
Ellis, E. Earle. *The Gospel of Luke.* New Century Bible. London, 1966.
Ellul, Jacques. *Violence.* New York, 1969.
Feil, E., and Weth, R. *Diskussion zur Theologie der Revolution.* Munich, 1969.
Foner, Phillip. *Selections from the Writings of Frederick Douglass.* New York, 1964.

Fletcher, Joseph. *Situation Ethics: The New Morality.* Philadelphia, 1966.

Flender, Helmut. *St. Luke, Theologian of Redemptive History.* London, 1967.

Galtung, Johan. *The European Community: A Super-Power in the Making.* Oslo-London, 1973.

Geiger, Theodor. *Ideologie und Wahrheit, eine soziologische Kritik des Denkens.* Berlin, 1968.

Geldenhuys, J. Norval. *The Gospel of Luke.* New London Commentary. London, 1969.

Gollwitzer, Helmut. *Die Kapitalistische Revolution.* Munich, 1974.

Gollwitzer, Helmut. *Die reiche Christen und der arme Lazarus—die Konzequenzen von Uppsala.* Munich, 1970.

Grier, William, and Cobbs, Price M. *Black Rage.* New York, 1972.

Gutiérrez, Gustavo. *A Theology of Liberation.* Maryknoll, New York, 1973.

Guardini, Romano. *De moderne mens en het probleem van de macht.* Utrecht, 1959.

Heering, G.J. *De Zondeval van her Christendom.* Utrecht, 1953.

Heering, H.J. *Ethiek der voorlopigheid.* Nijkerk, 1972.

Hengel, Martin. *Gewalt und Gewaltlosigkeit.* Stuttgart, 1971.

Hengel, Martin. *War Jesus Revolutionär?* Stuttgart, 1971.

Herzog, Frederick. *Liberation Theology.* New York, 1972.

Hoffmann, Klaus. *Das Kreuz und die Revolution Gottes.* Neukirchen: 1971.

Honig, A.G., Jr. *De kosmische betekenis van Christus.* Kamper Cahier No. 7. Kampen, 1969.

Honig, A.G., Jr. *Jezus Christus de Bevrijder, de inhoud van de missionaire verkondignig.* Kamper Cahier No. 25. Kampen, 1975.

Honig, A.G., Jr. *Meru en Golgotha.* Franeker, 1969.

Horsky, Vladimir. *Prag 1968. Systemveränderung und Systemverteidigung.* Studien zur Friedensforschung. Band 14. Stuttgart-Munich, 1975.

Houtart, F., and Rousseau, A. *The Church and Revolution.* Maryknoll, New York, 1971.

Howse, Ernest Marshall. *Saints in Politics: The Clapham Sect and the Growth of Freedom.* London, 1973.

Huet, P. *Het lot der zwarten in Transvaal. Mededeelingen omtrent slavernij en wreedheden in de Zuidafrikaansche republiek.* Utrecht, 1869.

Klapwijk, C. *Sociaal masochisme en chrisetelijk ethos.* Kampen, 1973.

Klapwijk, C. *Vreugde en lijden. Sociaal masochistische trekken in het christendom.* Kampen, 1974.

Kuitert, H.M. *Anders gezegd.* Kampen, 1970.

Kuitert, H.M. *De realiteit van het geloof.* Kampen, 1967.

Kuitert, H.M. *De spelers en het spel.* Baarn, 1970.

Kuitert, H.M. *Om en om.* Kampen, 1972.

Labuschagne, C.J. "De godsdienst van Israel en de andere godsdiensten." In *Wereld en Zending, tijdschrift voor missiologie,* no. 1, 1975.

Labuschagne, C.J. *Schriftprofetie en volksideologie.* Nijkerk, 1968.

Lehmann, Paul. *Ethics in a Christian Context.* New York, 1963.

Lehmann, Paul. *The Transfiguration of Politics: Jesus Christ and the Question of Revolution.* London, 1974.

Macht, Agressie, Geweld. *Kernvraag,* 1 and 2, December 1974, nos. 48, 49. *Macht.* Voordrachten gehouden in het kader van het Studium Generale van de Rijksuniversitetit Groningen. Haarlem, 1971.

Major, H.D.A., ed. *The Mission and Message of Jesus.* New York, 1947.

Manson, William. *Luke.* Moffat N. T. Commentary. London, 1930.

Matthews, Z.K., ed., *Responsible Government in a Revolutionary Age.* New York-London. 1966.

May, Rollo. *Power and Innocence: A Search for the Sources of Violence.* New York, 1962.

Míguez Bonino, José. *Doing Theology in a Revolutionary Situation.* Philadelphia, 1975.

Míguez Bonino, José. *Revolutionary Theology Comes of Age.* London, 1975.

Niebuhr, Reinhold. *Moral Man and Immoral Society.* New York, 1960.

Niebuhr, Reinhold. *The Nature and Destiny of Man II,* London, 1946.

Paoli, Arturo. *Freedom to be Free.* Maryknoll, New York, 1973.

Pedersen, J. *Israel, Its Life and Culture.* 2 vols. Copenhagen-London, 1926.

du Preez, A.B. *Eiesoortige Ontwikkeling tot Volksdiens.* Pretoria, 1959.

Pro Veritate. Monthly journal of the Christian Institute of Southern Africa.

Rasker, A.J. and Machovec, M. *Theologie und Revolution.* Evangelische Stimmen 41. Hamburg, 1969.

Randall, Peter. *A Taste of Power.* Johannesburg, 1973.

Rendtorff, T., and Rich, A., eds. *Humane Gesellschaft—Beitrage zu ihrer sozialen Gestaltung. Zum 70 Geburtstag von H.-D. Wendland.* Zurich, 1970.

Rengstorf, K.H. *Das Evangelium nach Lukas.* N.T. Deutsch. Göttingen, 1969.

Rhoodie, N.J., and Venter, H. *Apartheid.* Cape Town-Pretoria, 1960.

Rieger, P., and Strauss, J., eds. *Glauben und Gewalt.* Tützinger Texte 10. Munich, 1971.

Rijk, M.C. *Structuur, macht en geweld. Een analyse in het licht van een beschouwing over de mens in de huidige cultuur.* Bloemendaal, 1972.

Risk. "Incommunication." vol. 9, no. 2, 1973.

Richardson, Alan. *The Political Christ.* London, 1973.

Ridderbos, H.N. *The Coming of the Kingdom.* Philadelphia, 1962. Dutch original: *De Komist van het Koninkrijk.* Kampen, 1953.

Ridderbos, H.N. *Paulus, ontwerp van zijn theologie.* Kampen, 1967.

Ridderbos, S.J. "Het voorwerp vande liefde." In *Bezinning,* no. 4, 1963.

Ridderbos, S.J. "Liefde als gebod." In *Ned. Theol. Tijdschrift,* vol. 16, no. 4, April 1962.

Rothuizen, G.T. *Wat is theologie? Bonhoeffers laaste woord tot zijn studenten.* Kamper Cahier no. 13. Kampen, 1970.

Rothuizen, G.T. *Wat is ethiek?* Kampen, 1973.

Roux, Edward. *Time Longer than Rope. A History of the Struggle of the Black Man for Freedom in South Africa.* Madison, Wisconsin, 1963.

Schlatter, D.A. *Das Evangelium Lukas.* Stuttgart, 1931.

ter Schegget, G.H. *Het geheim van de mens.* Baarn, 1972.

ter Schegget, G.H. *Klassenstrijd en staking.* Baarn, 1974.

ter Schegget, G.H. *Partijgangers der Armen.* Baarn, 1970.

Schrey, H.H. *Entideologiserung als hermeneutisches Problem.* Tübingen, 1969.

Smalley, S., and Lindars, B., eds. *Christ and the Spirit in the New Testament: Essays in honour of C.F.D. Moule.* London, 1973.

Stanton, G.N. *The Message of Jesus in New Testament Preaching.* London, 1973.

Stern, E. Ed. *Macht door gehoorzaamheid. Een theologisch onderzoek naar de macht over mensen.* Baarn, 1973.

Stüttgen, Albert. *Kriterien einer Ideologiekritik.* Mainz, 1972.

Sundermeier, T., ed. *Church and Nationalism.* Johannesburg, 1975.

Swomley, J. *Liberation Ethics.* New York, 1972.

Theologische Stimmen aus Asien, Afrika und Lateinamerika. Band III. Munich, 1968.

Tillich, Paul. *The Courage to Be.* New Haven, 1952.

Tillich, Paul. *Love, Power and Justice.* New York, 1972.

Tödt, Ilse, ed. *Theologie im Konfliktfeld Südafrika. Dialog mit Manas Buthelizi.* Studien zur Friedensforschung Band 15. Stuttgart-Munich, 1976.

Vaughan, B.N.Y. *The Expectation of the Poor: The Church and the Third World.* London, 1972.

Vekuyl, J. *Breek de muren af! Over gerechtigheid in rassenverhoudingen.* Baarn, 1969.

Verkuyl, J. *De boodschap der bevrijding in deze tijd.* Kampen, 1973.

Verkuyl, J. *Inleiding in de nieuwere zendingswetenschap.* Kampen, 1975.

Verkuyl, J., ed. *Jezus Christus de Bevrijder en de voortgaande bevrijding van mensen en samen levingen.* Baarn, 1973.

Vos, J.S. "Vrijheid en emancipatie bij Paulus." In *Vox Theologica,* vol. 3, 1975.

de Vries, E., ed. *Man in Community.* London, 1966.

de Vries, J.L. "Sending en Kolonialisme in Suid-Wes Afrika." Unpublished dissertation, Protestantse Theologische Faculteit. Brussels, 1971.

Wendland, H.-D. *Ethik des Neuen Testaments.* NTD Erganzungsreihe 4. Göttingen, 1970.

Wendland, H.-D. *Sozialethik im Umbruch der Geseelschaft.* Göttingen, 1969.

Wiersinga, H. *De verzoening in de theologische diskussie.* Kampen, 1971.

Wiersinga, H. *Verzoening als verandering.* Baarn, 1972.

Wilson, Francis. *Migrant Labour in South Afrika.* Johannesburg, 1972.

Wilson, M., and Thompson, L., eds. *The Oxford History of South Africa.* 2 vols. London, 1973, 1974.

van Zuthem, H. *Gezag en Zeggenschap.* Kampen, 1968.

AUTHOR INDEX

184   Author Index

DATE DUE

GAYLORD			PRINTED IN U.S.A.